W9-AZI-597

The
Virgin
Homeowner's
Handbook

THE VIRGIN HOMEOWNER'S HANDBOOK

Hap Hatton
and Laura Torbet

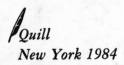

Quill
New York 1984

Copyright © 1984 by Hap Hatton and Laura Torbet

All rights reserved. No part of this book may be reproduced or utilized in any form or by any means, electronic or mechanical, including photocopying, recording or by any information storage and retrieval system, without permission in writing from the Publisher. Inquiries should be addressed to Quill, an imprint of William Morrow and Company, Inc., 105 Madison Avenue, New York, N.Y. 10016.

Library of Congress Catalog Card Number: 84-60449

ISBN: 0-688-03116-1

Printed in the United States of America

First Quill Edition

1 2 3 4 5 6 7 8 9 10

BOOK DESIGN BY PATTY LOWY

Preface

So you've bought a house. That's great news. If you're like us, owning a home will bring great rewards and pleasure and be a good investment to boot. But you may be in for a rude awakening when you realize the care and maintenance involved to keep your new roof over your head.

The Virgin Homeowner's Handbook came about soon after Laura Torbet purchased her first house. She learned the hard way that the roof gutters must periodically be cleared of leaves and debris and that the garden should be mulched in the fall. When the boiler shut down in the deep of winter, she didn't know there was a reset button to put it back in service again. Then there was the night of a power failure—though there was a flashlight in the house, there were no candles or kerosene lamps. And on it went, learning by experience every step of the way. She realized she needed a book about how to be a homeowner.

The VHH is different from the countless books available on everything from home repair to gardening and upholstering to home energy conservation. It is not an in-depth how-to book on a specific subject but the big picture, an overview of what needs to be done, when it needs to be done, and how to get it done—by yourself or by others.

Take it from us, someone who's never owned a house is often unaware of the things that need to be tended to and often ignorant of the most efficient way to get a simple task taken care of. *The VHH* takes you the novice homeowner in hand from the day you start to pack for the move, leads you all around the rooms and the grounds of your new house, showing you what needs to be done and when. In *The VHH* you'll learn how to do the simple repair and maintenance chores that aren't worth calling in a professional for. You'll get tips on getting to know the ins and outs of your new community. On how to ascertain that the basic systems of your new home are running smoothly and efficiently. On how to take care of the grounds around your house and the roof over it.

The purpose of *The Virgin Homeowner's Handbook* is not to make you a whiz-bang do-it-yourselfer but to educate you about what's involved in running a home, to give you a handy reference to consult, to help you evaluate the ways of getting the job done. We take into consideration that homeowners have different levels and varieties of skills, different budgets, and varying levels of desire to be involved with the intricacies of running and maintaining a home. There's something for everyone in *The VHH*!

It is our hope that *The Virgin Homeowner's Handbook* will help minimize the problems and maximize the very real enjoyments of owning your first home.

Acknowledgments

Because of the unique nature of this book, fellow homeowners provided the most assistance. Mark Cullingham and Michael Cressey had just purchased the old Senekes Lodge on Long Island and were most generous with the house and their experience. Doris and John Robert, the previous owners, moved right down the road and were encyclopedic in the hows, whens, and whys of homeowning. Mary and Brud Goldsmith get the good-neighbor award. Special thanks also go to Joyce and Ed Foster, Mr. Donnelly at the Center Moriches Free Public Library, Jim Landis and Alison Brown Cerier at William Morrow, Suzanne and Jennifer at Steph's, and Rene Graef and Jane Tenenbaum in Wisconsin.

Contents

Chapter 1

WHAT THE PREVIOUS OWNER CAN TELL YOU

The first and most essential step to responsible homeowning is to find out what makes your house tick. Before you start trying to figure out what will go where, before you pack a box, before you start filling out change-of-address labels—STOP! Set up an appointment with the previous owner of your new house. The information you obtain can save you aggravation, time, and money. For instance, knowing that the pipes to the outside faucets need to be drained in the winter can save you the headaches that come along when they freeze and burst. Save yourself from the panic that occurs when the furnace goes on the fritz during the worst blizzard in a decade, and as the temperature starts plunging you don't know what to do or whom to call. It's so simple to learn to troubleshoot the problem or to have taken the time to get the name of the person who has serviced the furnace for the past ten years and knows its idiosyncracies. And on it goes. It's one thing if the previous owner has moved across town—he or she may not like being disturbed but at least is available if you have to ask. It's another thing if the previous owner has moved to Honolulu.

Along with transferring a house to you, you must make sure that the previous owner also passes along the knowledge and know-how—in short, the benefit of his or her experience—to enable you to carry on in the house. It's up to you to make sure you learn all you can. A first house can seem intimidating, but an explanation and rundown of the place will make it seem less so. Knowing what to ask makes all the difference.

The material and information you'll need to gather fall into two categories:

Homework. These are the documents, instruction manuals, names, addresses, and records that need to be gathered, along with specific information that involves some thought or referring to records and files.

House tour. This involves questions and answers as you cover the premises.

DOCUMENTS AND MANUALS/NAMES, ADDRESSES, AND PHONE NUMBERS YOU'LL NEED

Give the owner a list of what you need and ask that it be gathered for you. Request the following:

- A complete set of blueprints (useful if major repairs or remodeling are ever done)

- Any plans for renovations that were never completed

- A plot survey map (this usually is an adjunct to your property deed)

- A property map of the lot showing exact locations of septic tanks or sewage lines, water lines, a well (if you have one), and any buried power or cable television lines. Draw one up if none is available. You probably can locate these on a copy of the plot survey map mentioned above (see also page 17).

- Wiring diagrams (for easier appraisal and/or upgrading of your electrical system)
- A history of the house, including any old photographs
- Instruction books, warranties, make and model numbers, suppliers, date purchased, and who to call for servicing on the following:
  — heating unit
  — air conditioning
  — hot-water heater
  — water pump (if municipality doesn't supply water)
  — refrigerator
  — freezer
  — stove
  — automatic garbage disposal (or garbage compactor)
  — attic fan
  — washing machine
  — drier
  — any other equipment purchased with the house (for example, a lawn mower)
- Names, addresses, and phone numbers of:
  — police department
  — fire department
  — rescue squad (if any)
  — the nearest doctor
  — the insurer of the house (and what type of policy, amount of coverage, and premium paid)
  — fuel oil supplier(s)
  — garbage collector (and days of pickup)
  — any contractors (including original) or other professionals who have worked on the house and what they did and when, including:
    electricians
    carpenters
    painters (you also need to know the type of paint used)
    plumbers
    roofers
    chimney cleaners

septic tank cleaners
locksmiths
exterminators
lawn mowing service
— recommended lumberyard and hardware/paint/home
supply store(s).

- With phone book Yellow Pages in hand and marked to sections, make notes and mark recommended local dealers (for instance, the previous owner's favorite appliance store, dry cleaners, furniture store, jeweler, lawyer, pharmacist, physician, restaurants, and any other facilities listed in Chapter 5: "Getting to Know the Territory").

A TOUR OF THE HOUSE AND GROUNDS

Before you set up an appointment for a house tour, read Chapter 8: "Around the House: How Everything Works and How You Can Make It Work More Efficiently." This is important—familiarizing yourself beforehand enables you to know what you're asking and understand what you're being told. It's also a good idea to carry along a notepad, tape cassette recorder, and shipping labels to attach to various switches and cutoff valves. If you don't have some way to record verbal instructions on a complicated system like the furnace, you're not going to remember them three months from now (or three days from now, for that matter). NOTE: During the tour, if it becomes readily apparent that the previous owner hasn't cleaned a filter or lubricated anything—in general, has done zero maintenance—it's essential you start *immediately* if you want things to last.

The Basement

- The heating system
  — How do you turn it on? Off?
  — Is there a reset button in case it shuts down? Has it ever?
  — Where is the filter? How often does it need cleaning? How do you change it?

— Does it have a pilot light? Do you turn it off in warm weather? How?

- The water system
  — If the house is hooked to a municipal system, where is the main shutoff valve? Where is the water meter?
  — If the house has its own well, pump, and pressure tank, how often have they been serviced? What kind of maintenance is required (lubricating, etc.), and what problems have occurred?
  — How are the pipes drained (in case you ever want to shut down the house for the winter)?
  — On the hot-water heater, where is the thermostat? The tap that sediment and mineral deposits can be drained from?
- The gas system
  — If gas—either municipal or bottled—is used for some essential service such as cooking, heating, or drying clothes, it is imperative you know the location of the main shutoff valve in case of an emergency.

The Kitchen

- The refrigerator: Where do you control the temperature? How often is defrosting necessary? How often do they clean the coils on the back and underneath (to keep the fridge operating at peak energy efficiency)? Is there a pan to catch any runoff underneath?
- The stove: Are the ovens self-cleaning? How? Are the controls self-explanatory? Does it have a timer? How does it work? Are there oven lights? Where do you turn them on? How do you change them?
- The exhaust fan: How do you turn it on? Clean the filter? Disassemble it to clean the blades and motor?
- The dishwasher: How do you operate it? Any special loading tips? Where do you put the detergent? Is there a drying cycle that can be shut off? Where is the filter that catches loose food and debris?

- The sink: How do you stop the drains? Are there aerators on the faucet?
- The garbage disposal: Where is the switch? Reset button? Have they ever had a clogged drain as a result of running certain substances through it (for instance, fibrous, pulpy asparagus stalks are prime cloggers)?

The Rest of the House

- The washing machine: Ask for a lesson in operating it. Where are the hot- and cold-water cutoff valves? Does the washing machine have a filter that traps lint and should be cleaned after each use?
- The drier: How do you use it? Where is the lint filter that should be cleaned after each use?
- Light switches: Get straight which switches control which lights (some lights are controlled by two switches) and which switches control wall outlets.
- The thermostat: Where is it? Any special instructions necessary to use it? At what temperature did they usually set it in the winter?
- The radiators: If the house is heated by radiators or circulating hot water, find out how to bleed the radiators or baseboard units. (See pages 171–72.)
- The registers: If the house is heated by hot air, where are the registers? How are they closed off? Which put out the most heat? The least?
- The fireplace: How do you open the damper? Who supplied wood? Kindling? Where was it stored?
- The air conditioning: Any special instructions for operating it? How are filters removed for cleaning? What other maintenance was done? If there are window units, did the previous owner remove them in winter? If so, how?
- Fans: If the house is not air-conditioned, what types of fans did they use? What was the fan setup they used for optimum comfort?

- Smoke detectors: Are there any smoke detectors installed? Where?
- Locks: Can all windows be locked?

The Attic

- How do you get to it?
- Is there a light there? Where do you turn it on?
- Is the attic ventilated? Where?
- The attic fan: Is there one? Where is the switch? Where do you oil it? What other maintenance is necessary?

Outside

- Storm windows: Are there any? Where are they stored? Is there a system for installing them? What goes where? Are they marked? Where? How are they fastened in place?
- Screens: ditto above
- The garage door: How do you open it? Lock it with a key from outside and without a key inside?
- Outside lights: Where are they? Where are the switches?
- Electric and water meters: Where are they? How often are they checked by the local utility?
- Fuel tank: What is the capacity? How long will a full tank last? Is there a gauge? If not, how do you measure?
- Outside faucets (sill cocks): Where? How are they drained in the winter?
- Antenna: What is it hooked up to? Where does the antenna wire feed into the house?
- Roof: Was there ever any problem with ice dams? (See page 189.)
- Crawl space: Where is the access? Is there more than one?
- Take the map of the property discussed on page 12 and pinpoint locations of sewage lines, water lines, and any buried underground power or cable television lines.

- Septic tank: Is there one? How do you get into it?
- Compost heap: Is there one? How old is it? What was general procedure in using it?
- Fertilizers: What kind did they use? Was a soil analysis ever taken? (See page 78.)
- Garden: Is there one? What grew or is growing there?
- Keys: Are any hidden outside?

Chapter 2

SAFETY AND SECURITY

RESIDENTIAL FIRES

Before you even move in, both the prevention of and the protection from fire must be top priorities of the virgin homeowner. Annually over half a million home fires kill in excess of ten thousand people and injure or disable over three hundred fifty thousand. Many of the casualties are children, and the majority of fires occur between midnight and 6:00 A.M., when most people are asleep. Take warning—it can happen to you.

According to the National Fire Protection Association,

most residential fires in this country are caused by the following:

- Smoking and matches (adults in the former case, children in the latter)
- Faulty electrical equipment and overloading inadequate or defective electrical wiring
- Inadequate flues and careless use of them
- Combustible materials too close to heaters, hot ashes, or coals
- Improper storage of flammable liquids

Fire-Prevention Inspection Tour

Make a house fire-prevention inspection tour. If you fall short in any of these areas, you are foolishly taking unnecessary risks.

- Are your ashtrays large enough and are they plentiful enough for the amount of smoking that takes place? If you smoke, are you always careful?
- Do you have a suitable, properly charged fire extinguisher for grease and electrical fires in the kitchen? Does everyone know how to use it? And is everyone aware that water should never be used to put out these fires?
- Do you have your furnace, hot water heater, and chimneys inspected or serviced regularly for safety? (You should—see pages 165–74 and 184–87.)
- Is the ceiling over the furnace covered for about five feet around with noncombustible material such as gypsum or cement board?
- If you have a wood stove, is it properly installed and regularly cleaned of creosote buildup?
- Does the fireplace have a screen?
- Are your home and service buildings free of litter and rubbish? Are there cluttered collections of stuff in the attic? In the garage? Under the house?
- Is the yard or lot free of weeds, tall grass, brush, and trash?

- Are flammable liquids such as gasoline for the lawn mower, barbecue fire starter, and paint remover properly stored in metal, airtight containers and used with caution?

- Is there anything combustible above or around a heater, water heater, or the pilot light of a cookstove?

- Are oily rags discarded or kept in metal containers (where they could spontaneously combust)?

- Is house wiring adequate? (See pages 152–57.) Have you had it checked lately?

- Are all electrical cords in good repair? (See pages 115–20.)

- Are you putting a strain on your electrical system (see pages 152–57) by:
  — using flimsy dime-store extension cords on heavy appliances such as electric irons, space heaters, or electric tools?
  — "overfusing"—that is, putting in heavier and heavier fuses and overloading your electrical system? (For most households the safe circuit limit is fifteen amperes.)
  — putting pennies behind your fuses to get them to carry a bigger load?

- Have you allowed proper ventilation space around television and stereo equipment?

- Are chafing dishes, fondue pots, and the like protected by metal trays underneath that would catch any alcohol overflow?

- Have you taught your children to respect fire and not to play with matches?

- Are you careful not to store cookies and goodies above the stove, where the kids might accidentally turn on the stove getting to them?

- If you live in an area with frequent thunderstorms:
  — Is your TV antenna properly grounded? (Otherwise lightning can be conducted directly into the house by the lead-in wires.)
  — Is your house equipped with a lightning protection sys-

tem? (Houses located on hilltops or on flat plains are especially vulnerable to being struck.)

• If you are doing any remodeling work, are you inquiring about the flammability characteristics of all building materials, including insulation, paints, wood and imitation wood paneling, curtains, and carpets?

The Importance of Having Smoke Detectors

Where there's fire, there's smoke, and where there's a smoke detector, there is the probability that family members will be alerted and evacuated from a burning house and that the fire department will be notified faster.

Smoke, not flames, is the number one killer in fires. Many home fires smolder for hours before they burst into open flames. This incomplete combustion releases large quantities of toxic gases, especially carbon monoxide. If you're asleep when the gas enters your room, you'll never wake up—unless a smoke detector wakes you up.

What's Available?   Two types of detectors are on the market, photoelectric and ionization chamber. Here are the differences:

Photoelectric	*Ionization Chamber*
detects smoke by "seeing it" in much the same way eyes do, by means of light reflected by particles of smoke	contains a small radiation source that rarefies air and produces smoke-sensitive ions
over twenty *minutes* faster detecting slow, smoldering fires (like those started by a cigarette dropped on bedding or furniture, which are the more common household fires)	twenty to thirty seconds quicker detecting fast-burning fire (a few seconds can mean the difference between life and death in this kind of fire)

- An alarm combining both types of detector would seem ideal, but *Consumer Reports* says that their actual performance is less so and that the combined price of the top-rated ionization and top-rated photoelectric detectors is less than the cost of a single combination unit. *CR* recommends using at least one of each, placing an ionization detector just outside bedroom doors and a photoelectric model either in or near living quarters (where slow-burning fires tend to start).

A Few More Facts

- Detectors are equipped with a test button, lever, or switch so you can check whether or not battery and alarm are working. Dirt could prevent the unit from detecting smoke even though the button test would indicate otherwise. Check an ionization detector with actual smoke from a burning candle and a photoelectric detector with smoke from a freshly extinguished candle or match.

- To avoid frequent false alarms, do not install a detector in a kitchen, close to a fireplace, near a heating unit, or in a garage.

- *Consumer Reports* debates the safety of sleeping with the bedroom door closed, as many detector instructions advise. A closed door could mute an outside alarm, and hinder detection of a fire that started in the bedroom itself.

- The National Bureau of Standards claims the radioactive material in the ionization detector is not a health hazard, but these detectors do put out very minimal amounts of radiation that are absorbed into the body, and the manufacturers insist that detectors be returned to them rather than be thrown in the garbage. (The U.S. Nuclear Regulatory Commission says if you hugged one close to you eight hours a day for a year, you'd receive a tenth as much radiation as a plane passenger flying from New York to Los Angeles.)

- Whatever you buy, it should be approved by a major testing laboratory such as Underwriters Laboratories (UL) or by Factory Mutual Laboratories (FM).

• For more information, write "Smoke Detectors," National Fire Prevention and Control Administration, Commerce Department, Washington, DC 20230.

Fire Extinguishers and Fire Fighting

Although fighting a fire should be a third priority after getting everybody out and after turning in an alarm, you can fight small fires.

• To understand how fire can be controlled, let's start at the beginning. Three ingredients must be combined for a fire to burn:
  — air (oxygen)
  — fuel (something that will burn)
  — heat (something to ignite and to continue burning)

• If any of these factors is removed from a fire, it will go out!

• There are three classes of fire:

Class	Involves	Best Extinguishing Agent
A	ordinary nonliquid combustibles such as wood, textile, paper, plastic, rubber	water
B	flammable liquids such as grease, oil, gasoline, paint, and paint solvent	cut off oxygen supply; in case of kitchen grease fire, smother fire with frying pan lid or baking soda (not flour, which can explode, and never water, which can splatter and spread the flames)
C	live electrical wiring and equipment, such as appliances connected to household wiring	dry chemical fire extinguisher (never use water because of risk of electric shock)

- Fire extinguishers are classified according to the class and size of fire they can put out.
  - A-rated extinguishers: A 1A extinguisher must be able to stop a test fire of fifty pieces of wood measuring two inches by two inches by twenty inches. A 2A must be able to handle twice as much. (Water, and lots of it, still remains the most effective agent against Class A fires.)
  - B-rated extinguishers: A 1B has to put out 3¼ gallons of naphtha (a very highly combustible and volatile liquid) burning in a 2½-square-foot pan.
  - C-rated extinguishers: These have no numerical prefix; the unit is guaranteed safe for electrical fires because the extinguishing material does not conduct electricity.

Some Recommendations

- *Consumer Reports* recommends having at least two 1A:10BC extinguishers in smaller homes—one in the kitchen and one in a sleeping or living area. Larger homes should be equipped with additional units in both garage and basement, and one of them ought to be rated 2A.

- Extinguishers should be hung on the wall near the door that you most often use to enter the room in which a fire is most likely to start (kitchen, workshop, etc.). Don't place the fire extinguisher too close to the most likely source of fire.

- An extinguisher must be recharged once it has been discharged, no matter how briefly.

- Like smoke detectors, buy only those fire extinguishers approved by the Underwriters Laboratories (UL) or by Factory Mutual Laboratories (FM).

Preparing For and in Case of Fire

- Set up an escape plan. Children often panic, hiding in closets or under beds, and are helpless to save themselves unless they've been instructed what to do. Pay particular attention to escape from bedrooms, where children and elderly or infirm family members are most likely to be trapped by fire.

- Instruct family members not to waste time getting dressed or collecting prized possessions. Speed is essential in escaping from a fire.

- Upstairs windows with no roof or landing outside should be equipped with a fire escape ladder. A heavy knotted rope will serve. Have either tied to something solid such as a radiator or an eye hook screwed into a wall stud.

- Plan where you will meet after escape so an accurate head count can be taken and no one risks going back inside for someone who is already safe.

- Make sure that every family member knows how to test a door. Flinging open a door can kill you if there's an inferno on the other side. Apply this test: Put your hand on the door panel and knob. If either is warm, keep the door closed and use an alternate escape route. If not, brace foot and hip against the door and open cautiously to prevent super-heated air from blowing it open. If there's no hot air or smoke, it is probably safe to pass through.

- If a door is open and you decide to exit through a window, close the door before you use the window. Fires should be given as little fresh air as possible.

- As you escape from a smoke-filled room, crouch low with a cloth or handkerchief over your mouth and nose. Keep your head about eighteen inches above the floor. Poisonous gases accumulate near the ceiling and floor of a burning building. The cloth over the face will help relieve some of the irritating effects of inhaled smoke, although it won't filter out poisonous gases. Avoid deep breathing.

- Phone the fire department after everyone has been alerted and evacuated. Getting out is the important thing—fires can literally race through a house and trap you while you are dialing.

THE OTHER THREAT—BURGLARY

No resident in this country is safe from burglary, and the crime rate is soaring. The old days of going off and leaving the house unlocked are over. Burglars now operate as much by day as by night, and they don't take off for holidays—break-ins reach their peak on Christmas and at New Year's. And burglars read the newspapers—while you're at a wedding or a funeral, they may visit your house.

General Rules to Follow

- Avoid leaving notes on the door saying you're away, even if it's for only a half hour.
- Keep unused doors locked at all times.
- Door hinges should be mounted on the inside of doors rather than on the outside. If they're already outside, make sure the pins cannot be removed.
- Garage doors that open with "Open Sesame" ease from your car can also easily be opened by a hep burglar. The best garage door lock is a box with a key that, when inserted and turned, opens the door.
- Ladders should never be left in plain sight. Put them away.
- Check the reputation or references of any new people working in or around your house.
- Any plate-glass picture windows or sliding doors should be made of reinforced glass.
- Protect *yourself*, too—and your family. A peephole in the door is necessary these days so you can see who's ringing the doorbell before you open the door.
- Be wary of suspicious callers who actually may be casing your house, and think twice before accepting any suspicious invitations—burglars have been known to send free tickets, then rob the house during showtime.

The Vacation or Weekend Home (or When You're Away on Vacation)

- Let your neighbors and local police or sheriff's department know when you'll be in residence.

- Have someone collect your mail or have the post office hold it.

- If you have an extra car, leave it conspicuously parked.

- Arrange to have the lawn mowed.

- Don't leave all your window shades down. This advertises that you're away.

- Lights operated by timers are better suited for security than the automatic lights that go on at sunset and off at sunrise. A savvy burglar can spot the latter. Timers can turn lights on and off, even at different times different nights. Several low-wattage indoor lights make the house look more occupied than one high-wattage one.

- A radio hooked to a timer—with or without a light—is a good safeguard.

- If you're going away on vacation, stop all newspapers, milk, and other deliveries.

- For more specifics on vacation or weekend homes, see Chapter 10.

Locks, the First Line of Defense

Locks have two component parts: the lock cylinder (where you put the key) and the bolt on the edge of the door (which slides into a slot on the doorjamb called a strike and keeps the door from opening). There are basically two types of locks: a spring latch or key-in-knob type and a dead bolt, which must be operated manually with a key or thumb turn. Dead bolts offer better protection than spring-latch locks, which can be sprung easily by burglars. There are many versions of each. Here are some pointers.

- When buying any keyed lock, get the five-pin, pickproof, cylinder type. It derives its name from the row of five locking pins the key lines up before it turns and moves the bolt or latch.

- Make sure the wood screws that come with the lock are long enough for secure attachment. Most intruders use force instead of lock-picking skill for entering.

- For any doors containing glass, use double-cylinder dead bolts that are operated on both sides by keys, which should never be left in the locks.

- All outside doors, including the cellar door, should be equipped with cylinder-type dead-bolt locks, with the strike protected by metal. The bolt should go far enough into the strike so it can't be forced. Don't rely on safety chains inside; they can be sheared by the force of a 175-pound man.

- As a safeguard, have locks, cylinders, and keys changed when you move into your new place. On finer cylinders you can have the locksmith change the key combination and provide you with new keys, thereby saving the cost of a new cylinder. Or retain existing locks and add new ones.

- When installing a new lock, make the lock picker's job more difficult by mounting it above eye level.

- Don't put identification of any sort on your keys.

- Don't rely on locks that can be opened by a master key.

Burglar Alarms

For years burglar alarms have been commonplace in business establishments. The rise in home break-ins, however, has led to the manufacture of alarm systems with the homeowner's needs in mind. Systems are being developed with great rapidity. You should be prepared to spend upward of two hundred dollars for one. First answer the following questions to evaluate your needs:

- What am I protecting?

- Where are the vulnerable spots in my home?

- Is protection more important while I'm at home (when my presence hopefully should thwart intruders) or while I'm away (and the coast is clear for a burglar)?

- Should the alarm be activated before or after entry?

- Whom do I want an activated alarm to notify? Just me? The neighbors? The police?

The two basic alarm systems

Perimeter	Motion
consists of magnetic sensors attached to windows and outside doors	consists of small boxes that detect movement within the house; can monitor critical areas such as hallways, stairs, and room entrances
detects intruder in act of entering	doesn't operate until intruder is in the house
won't stop intruder climbing in through a broken window instead of raising sash	can be set off by anything that moves, including pets, rustling curtains, even air currents from radiators or air conditioners
allows free movement within house when system is turned on	can inhibit movement within home
sensors can be wired to central control unit, or wireless cigarette-pack-size transmitters can emit low-power signals to central control box	works by variety of mechanisms: sensitive to infrared (heat) or light or project microwave or ultrasonic waves
involves more work in installing; some systems are elaborately wired	easier to set up, and many are simple to move around

Perimeter	*Motion*
relatively inexpensive, says *Consumer Reports:* $190 to $284 for a six-room house with two outside doors, eleven double-hung windows, and no basement; wireless perimeter system could run $787 to $1407 for the same house, though some doubling up of sensors could lower the price (because double-hung windows need two sensors, the cost of either the wired or the wireless system can be cut by closing the upper sash permanently with long screws)	costs from $55 to $237 per unit; two or three, properly placed and aimed, can adequately protect a small house Note: Motion alarms can also function as a perimeter system by surrounding a house, but the conditions must be right to prevent nuisance alarms

- Other Types of Alarms
  — "Panic buttons"—just that—placed next to your front door or bed and usually wired to local police headquarters.
  — "Video sentinel"—*Consumer Reports* considers these more suitable for monitoring children in swimming pools. Who has time to monitor their own home twenty-four hours a day?
  — "Welcome lights"—Turn on outdoor lights automatically when anyone (or anything) approaches its infrared sensor. A photoelectric cell prevents the system from working during the day.

- When activated, alarm systems can:
  — sound a siren, horn, or other noise-making device and/or
  — automatically dial the local police and/or fire depart-

ments and transmit a taped message that a burglary is taking place at your address.

Note: Check with your local police department about any restrictions on automatic dialing devices. Because there are so many false alarms in some areas you may have to employ the services of a private twenty-four-hour monitoring service (check the Yellow Pages of the phone directory under "burglar"). Your activated alarm will dial the service, which in turn calls your house. If there's no answer or whoever answers cannot give a secret code word, the service calls the police.

Shop Carefully

- Security problems vary from house to house, and a system that's right for one may be wrong for another.
- Deal with a reputable dealer. Your Better Business Bureau can tell you if any complaints have been filed against the dealer you've picked.
- Check the effectiveness of the device or system you're considering with any of the following:
  — the local police
  — *Consumer Reports*
  — someone who is living with a similar system. A reputable dealer won't hesitate to refer you to his customers.
- Pay attention to the power source of your alarm. Automatic recharging batteries are best because they'll operate even during a power failure or if a burglar gets to your power source (fuse box, etc.).
- Be sure to check that any equipment you may want to add to your system will be compatible with what you're purchasing now.

Operation Identification—Tagging Your Possessions

Operation Identification has proven itself to be an effective public-service campaign that has helped cut down on residential burglaries. The plan works like this:

- Engrave your driver's license number on valuable possessions that burglars find most appealing—TV sets, stereos, cameras, electric tools, jewelry, etc. Tag larger items (see fig. 2-1).

- Then advertise that you've done so. Put stickers (see fig. 2-2) on your home's front door and on other obvious places.

Fig. 2-1

Fig. 2-2

This helps foil thieves in three ways: (1) If they get caught with stolen property they can't plead that it is their own. (2) Your possessions are now easily identifiable, which means that "fences" who traffic in stolen property are not so eager to buy or resell them. The thief gets stuck with the goods when what he really wants is cash. (3) The stickers may discourage a thief from breaking in at all.

- For their "action kit" write to Operation Identification, Acme Burgess, Route 83, Grayslake, IL 60030, or contact your local police department to see if there is a similar program available in your locale.

HOUSE INSURANCE—PROTECTING YOUR INVESTMENT

You don't want to find out how underinsured you are the hard way, so be thorough when investigating homeowners' insurance, and review your policy at least annually. Even inflation and rising property values will make you underinsured.

Your real-estate agent, banker, lawyer, and new neighbors are good sources of recommendations of reputable insurance agents. Often it's a good idea to insure with the previous owners' agent. At least examine the type of policy and coverage they had and begin there. To get you started we'll give you the types of policies available and the jargon you'll encounter.

- Burglary and theft insurance: insures stolen property. Some policies include an off-premises clause that protects against theft anywhere in the world.

- Deductibles: the amount you pay on each claim or accident before the insurance company will begin payment. Note: The higher the deductible you choose, the lower the premium you pay.

- Extended coverage: takes your policy beyond protection from fire and lightning to protection from wind, hail, explosion, riot, smoke, vehicles, and aircraft. In most cases actual cash value (not market value) will be reimbursed as opposed to depreciated value.

- Fire insurance: Besides covering full damage by fire and lightning, it also should cover miscellania such as water damage and vandalism. Check to see what extended coverage includes.

- Homeowner's policy: a "package" policy that usually combines property, burglary, fire, and liability.

- Liability insurance: The Avon lady slips as she's ringing your bell. Liability insurance protects you when she sues. A personal liability policy should cover medical payments as well as protect you if you accidentally damage the property of others or hurt someone.

- Property insurance: extended coverage (see above) against loss or damage to your property. Doesn't include personal liability.

The Home Inventory

Once you're settled in, take the time to inventory your home. Think how difficult it would be to remember exactly what you had if you were to lose it.

- A room-by-room format is best; try to establish a value for everything.

- Photographs are an excellent way to catalog the contents of your home, and they'll also help you remember by association things you may have forgotten to add or things you've subsequently added.

- Once you've made up an inventory, stash it in a safe place like a safe-deposit box or a fireproof container. And revise it whenever you make any significant changes in your home.

- Most insurance companies have homeowners' inventory booklets or forms available.

Chapter 3

THE MOVING EXPERIENCE

Moving is always a major undertaking, but with planning and preparation, it is manageable. By following the guidelines and schedules in this chapter, you'll avoid much of the anxiety, frustration, overwork, and property damage that often accompany a moving experience. The more effort invested ahead of time to make your move go smoothly, the less likely any problems will turn up to dampen the excitement of settling into your first home.

THE VHH *MOVING TIMETABLE*

Six to Eight Weeks Before

- Start a moving notebook. This will be your reference book for the next two months. All inventories, lists, phone numbers, etc., should go here. Keep this notebook nearby. Things will keep popping into your mind. Write them down!
  - Make separate lists of items you want to sell, to throw away, and to give away. Call the Salvation Army to take

away things that have good use left in them, or drop the items off at your church or local Goodwill. (If you make an evaluation and keep the list of items donated, at least part of your contribution is tax-deductible.) Another alternative is to have a garage sale, then give away what you don't sell.

— Make special lists of your most valuable and fragile possessions. As will be pointed out later, especially valuable items should be packed by the movers so they are responsible in case of damage.

— Take the measurements of the front door of the new house and start a list of your bulkiest possessions. Is there anything that might not fit? Anything you're unsure of should be cleared with the movers.

• Get change-of-address kit from the post office. Use it to change subscription addresses and to notify credit card companies, charge accounts, insurance companies, the motor vehicle office, banks, and other correspondents such as friends and relatives. It takes six to eight weeks to get your addresses changed with most big organizations. If a current mail label is available, enclose it with your change of address to help keypunchers get all the right information. This is also your opportunity to arrange with the post office to have your mail forwarded as of your moving date.

• Begin to use up foods in your freezer and the nonperishables and canned goods in your pantry. It's smarter to eat them than to move them.

• Begin to check up on the available movers. Have their representatives come to make an estimate (in writing). See the sections on choosing and dealing with movers later in this chapter (pages 43–46).

• Either from the mover or elsewhere, get packing crates, boxes, and wardrobes. Movers prefer cartons with flaps so the boxes can be sealed. Liquor stores are a good source for these; supermarkets usually cut off the tops of their cardboard boxes. Make sure cartons are a manageable size. If you'll need new garbage pails and kitchen trash pails in the new house, buy them now. They come in handy to pack things such as clothes, plates, and small breakables. Don't forget that laundry baskets, hampers, buckets, and other such things make excellent containers for moving. Also buy sealing tape and a good marking pen. Start saving newspapers for packing.

• Order any new furniture and appliances, and arrange delivery to the new home.

• If you're moving from an apartment, arrange the use of the service elevator on moving day.

• Make sure that you know exactly what fixtures, fittings, and appliances are going to be left in your new home. All of this should have been carefully spelled out in the contract to buy. Now is the time to double-check, especially if you're presently renting. You don't want to arrive to find bare wires hanging from the ceiling, no doorknobs, and no clothes rods in the closet.

• Plan yourself a farewell party.

One Month Before

• Find out if your local utilities will disconnect your major appliances if you're taking them with you. Movers won't unhook your gas stove or any electric appliances that are wired directly into main switches, nor will they disconnect a TV antenna or take an air conditioner out of a window. If your utilities don't provide this service, you'll need to make other arrangements. No matter who's going to do it, whether it be a plumber or the appliance dealers from whom you bought them, this is the time to make the appointment. (Think twice about moving major appliances. It's better to sell them independently or as part of the house or apartment.)

• Start packing items that won't be needed immediately, such as clothing out of season, books, and china. Label contents of cartons, where they go in the new house, and the urgency with which they need to be unpacked. Record this information in your notebook.

- Don't pack anything you don't like or that's readily replaceable—such as the bricks you've been using for your bookcases. And don't take an excess of clothes that are unsuitable for a new climate.

- Be sure to tape screws and any other miscellania to the objects to which they belong.

- It is easier to clean, paint, wallpaper, sand floors, etc., in an empty house. If you can arrange it so the owners of your new house are gone far enough in advance of your moving in, it will give you a better opportunity to prepare the place.

Two Weeks Before

- Get together with the previous owner of your new residence for keys, operating instructions, documents, and everything else covered in "Chapter 1: What the Previous Owner Can Tell You."

- If at all possible, set up a day when you can clean the new place after it's been vacated. It's much easier to clean an empty house than to move in and then attempt it. (See pages 48–50.)

- Assuming your local dry cleaner has three- or four-day service, now is the time to send out any items such as drapes, slip covers, and clothing that you want cleaned before the move.

- Confirm disconnection of any major appliances you're taking with you. Make sure the workers will be showing up a day or two before you vacate.

- Arrange a date for phone and utilities to be connected at your new residence. You and the previous tenant might arrange to have the account transferred to your name rather than terminated. If this is not possible, you can avoid paying a deposit by using the utility companies at your old address as references, even if they're out-of-state.

- Arrange fuel delivery at your new house.

- If your children are too young to be put to work, simplify your life by arranging with a friend, neighbor, or day-care center to take them for the day. Parcel out the pets as well; however, if you can't, on moving day they can be put in the bathroom or in some other holding pen so they won't disturb the movers and the excitement won't disturb them.

- Don't leave town without settling bills with local merchants and closing local charge accounts.

- Return all borrowed items, especially library books.

- Get back all tools and equipment you lent to neighbors and friends.

- Confirm the moving date with the movers.

One Week Before

- Phone your utilities that you're moving and want your services cut off. Follow this up with a card. Tell them on the phone that you want written confirmation of your termination. Otherwise, you may be slapped, even years from now, with an outrageous bill for services in a house you vacated years ago.

- Stop services such as garbage pickup, newspaper, and milk delivery. Start them up at the new place.

- Arrange fuel delivery to be stopped at your old residence. For closing purposes, assess the amount of fuel on hand.

- Try to find out what your new phone number will be and arrange to have phone calls forwarded to it. It's also highly important that once you are established in your new home you make sure that directory information has your new listing and that when you dial your old number you get a correct referral.

- Make an appointment to have the appliances you're moving hooked up when they get to your new place.

- Organize a moving plan. Assign a code letter to each room of the new house and label all of your big items to indicate the room to which each should be moved.

- Make plans for the first few days in your new home. Know where people are going to sleep and eat. And allow for foul-ups, especially late delivery of your household effects. Pack a couple of cartons with the following essentials and transport them in your car in case the movers are seriously delayed.
  — Toiletries such as toothbrushes, toothpaste, bath soap, shaving gear, shampoo, etc. (the same as you'd take on a weekend trip)
  — Towels, washcloths, a shower curtain, toilet paper
  — Snacks (including coffee or tea and brewing equipment) and kitchen utensils (a sharp knife, forks, spoons, knives, plates, glasses, cups, etc.)
  — Bedding
  — Pajamas
  — A couple of changes of clothes
  — Hangers
  — Cleaning equipment (including paper towels and dish-washing soap)
  — Trash bags
  — A flashlight and extra lightbulbs
  — Bandages, antiseptic, aspirin

- Send your books and other dense nonbreakables by common carrier. You'll save a good deal if you ship this kind of thing via train, bus, or UPS rather than having the very dense weight added to that of your furniture and other household goods.

- Plan menus for the first meals in your new home, and take food with you. The other alternative is to know a good nearby restaurant.

- Cancel memberships in local clubs and religious institutions.

- Close bank account or accounts and arrange for transfer of funds.

- Gather up all sets of keys to the old house and arrange to hand over all but three sets—one for your pocket, one for another responsible person, and one for the movers' foreman. These people should have sets of keys to the new house as well.

- Inform police and neighbors if your old house is to be empty. Leave a few lights on.

The Big Day

- Keep a variety of drinks around. Don't let the movers whisk off the kettle and coffee pot and paper cups until everything else is on the truck.

- Empty the fridge and store perishables in a cooler or the washing machine. Defrost and leave the refrigerator open when you depart.

- Supervise the packing and loading of special-care items such as valuables, heirlooms, and fragile pieces. If possible, have them assembled in one place.

- Check cellar, attic, closets, garage, yard, garden shed, and clothesline for leftover items.

- Take your time when you sign the lists the movers' foreman will press upon you. He may claim that he has another job to get to or try to rush you in some other way. Those are his problems. Your problem is to make certain that the lists reflect every item you've packed. If anything is missing or broken, those lists are your first step in settling the dispute, so make sure you understand the movers' codes and you agree on the condition of the goods. One way to track what goes onto the truck is to have a responsible family member or friend check off in your notebook everything that is loaded. Then compare that with the bill of lading. When you're surrounded by movers moving every which way with your boxes and furniture, it's nearly impossible to keep up with it yourself.

- Broom-sweep the old place.

- Turn down the thermostat.

- If you're moving during the winter and your old home is going to stand vacant for a few days or longer, make sure you drain the tanks and pipes after the water has been turned off. Turn off the heater, too. Be sure to leave a note about what you've done. Then dust off your hands, lock the door, and move on.

At the New House

- Get there before the movers do. Label all the rooms according to your floor plans and lists.

- Check to make sure the utilities are working. If you have trouble, you'll find the numbers in your notebook. Stay calm when you complain and make sure to get everyone's name. Don't hesitate to ask for a supervisor or department manager. If you used a real-estate agent to find your home, that agent may be able to handle your initial utility problems.

- Introduce yourself to the neighbors if you haven't met them already. They can be an immediate help if you have questions about your new neighborhood.

CHOOSING A MOVER

- If you are moving within your own state or city, the best way to choose a mover is to ask among your neighbors and to check with the Better Business Bureau. (See page 230.)

- If you're moving out of state, your mover will be regulated by the Interstate Commerce Commission, the ICC. There are local offices in Atlanta, Boston, Chicago, Fort Worth, Los Angeles, Miami, New York, Philadelphia, and San Francisco. All of these offices have computer terminals that allow you to call for up-to-date information on twenty-five hundred interstate movers. This will let you know how often they get the shipments to their destinations on time, how often their estimates are under the actual cost of the move, and how often their customers complain.

- Have the movers whose reputations seem good look at your house. Remember that the estimate isn't binding, since the move is charged by weight. This is why reputation is so important. Make sure you show the mover everything, from the old trunk in the attic and band saw in the basement to the garden house out back, the kids' sleds in the garage, and the filing cabinet in the den. Don't assume that you'll be able to get rid of things; let the mover include everything, and you'll get a more accurate estimate.

- Your mover must supply you with a copy of "Summary of Information for Shippers of Household Goods," but if you want to bone up on the information in it before you begin to get estimates, write to ICC, Household Goods Branch, Washington, DC 20423 for a free copy.

DEALING WITH MOVERS

- Go over your floor plans with the foreman of the moving crew. Give instructions to him only. While moving in, aside from double-checking on the stereo and other expensive and fragile items, keep a low profile. It's hard to be on hand and yet stay out of things, but that's the wisest approach.

- Some veterans of several moves swear that it's wise to budget a generous tip. Give half of it in advance to the crew and hint that the other half will be there at the end of the day if all goes well. Figure ten dollars per person per day, with an additional ten dollars for the foreman. On interstate moves, however, tipping is illegal. It may also be illegal in your state. Get it straight by asking about tips when you're getting estimates.

- Go to the weighing of your goods or send someone you can trust. The weight should include the van, driver, dollies, and moving equipment as well as your goods. It should not include four or five two-hundred-pound moving men.

- If you suspect some sort of shenanigans, you can insist on a reweighing. The mover must do it. He may charge you twenty or thirty dollars, but if the reweighing comes in more than 120 pounds lower than the original weighing or 25 percent more than the estimate, you don't have to pay the reweighing fee.

- If there isn't a weight scale, the mover may charge you at a rate of seven pounds to the square foot. This works to your advantage only if you're moving books and paper.

- Get copies of both weight tickets. There's one for the tare (the empty weight of the truck and equipment) and another for the gross (the weight of the truck loaded with your goods). Your copies should match the originals.

- If your goods are shipped with other people's, ask for the vehicle load manifest, which indicates what percentage of the entire load is chargeable to you. The driver must show this to you, and he must carry it with him. Check the tare, gross, and net of your goods on the manifest against these figures on your weight tickets and bill of lading. These numbers must match the corresponding numbers on the vehicle load manifest. If there's an inconsistency, report it to the ICC unless the mover corrects the figures right away.

- The mover must list all your goods and their condition. It is crucial that you examine the inventory carefully to see that it accurately describes your goods' condition. Keep a list of anything that gets broken or damaged while being packed. Also note things packed with a different room's furnishings, or otherwise misplaced; this will make it easier for you to check things at the other end. Read the movers' code and then go over the inventory. Have the foreman change the notation on any item you disagree with. If the foreman won't make the change, you've still got your own note on the original.

- Be sure to get a bill of lading. It states the delivery place, where to reach you, and the terms of liability for loss or damage.

- If you have antiques or any other especially valuable goods to be moved, list them on the bill of lading yourself. Movers deny liability for these items if they aren't specified and listed on the bill of lading.

- Check the terms of payment. Usually you'll have to pay by cash, certified check, or money order. If the charges exceed the estimate by more than 10 percent, you can pay the estimate plus 10 percent, then pay the balance within fifteen days. (Have two separate certified checks drawn to cover this possibility—one for the estimate, one for the estimate plus 10 percent. Keep enough cash on hand to cover the difference between these two sums.) This is the time to demand a reweighing if the figures seem inordinately high.

- When your goods are unloaded, examine them carefully! Note every problem—items missing, damaged goods, whatever. Your claim will be based on the notes you have made on the inventory upon both loading and unloading.

Chapter 4

SETTLING IN

Remember the last cardboard box packed? The one with the kettle and coffee pot? Unpack it first and brew yourself a cup of tea or coffee. You've arrived. Now what?

First, attempt to make the place habitable with concentrated activity. Then start taking care of business around town or at work and put in two to four hours a day on the unpacking and small jobs around the house. It will all get done slowly and surely . . . and properly.

ORGANIZE FROM THE START

The VHH insists that organization is the name of the game. For instance, put the everyday dishes in a cabinet near the dishwasher so that every time you unload it you don't have to carry the dishes across the kitchen. Pots and pans should be stored next to the stove, where they're used. And when something needs to go upstairs, don't make a special trip. Set it by the stairs. Then when you're headed that way, gather up items that have accumulated. Especially in these days of endless putting things away, make every trip count. Before you leave one room and head for another, ask yourself, "What can I take where?" It's a good habit to develop, even after you've settled in.

Throughout the house, set up organized work centers that include the utensils and supplies needed to perform in that area. The closet with the cleaning supplies should be strategically located. Set up another one upstairs if you have a big house. Make your laundry room into a complete clothing-care center where they can be sorted and ironed as well as mended. Even taking the time to buy good doormats will reduce the amount of cleaning later needed throughout the house. Organization saves time and energy. You've taken on a big responsibility with your first house; make it easier on yourself.

PREPARATORY CLEANING

The closing agreement says the previous owner is supposed to leave the house broom-clean. Hopefully you've had the opportunity to visit and prepare the house. Repair work and cleaning are easier when the place is empty. Before you move in is the perfect time for any floor sanding and wall painting. Even window cleaning is simpler when there are no drapes to contend with.

If you haven't had a chance to clean the new place, the general rule is to make sure nothing is put away into an area that hasn't been thoroughly cleaned. This, of course, involves cleaning as you go, but it beats cleaning closets or cupboards later, when you have to remove everything. After cleaning, close cabinet and closet doors to keep out dust you stir up elsewhere. You should arrive at the new house with all of the following (If you can, leave any cleaning gear you can do without at the new place):

— A good broom
— Dust pan and small whisk broom
— Vacuum cleaner (make sure the bag is empty)
— Mop and pail
— Household cleaners, such as ammonia, detergent, and cleanser
— Floor wax
— Shampoo/polisher (you can rent one)—for shampooing carpets or polishing floors)
— Rags/sponges/paper towels
— A step ladder
— Toilet brush and bowl and tank cleaner
— Window cleaner (a mixture of white vinegar, ammonia, and water works as well as Windex)
— Shelf paper
— Newspapers
— Trash bags
— A picnic lunch

- Weather permitting, open all windows. Circulating air will remove much of the dust you stir up and keep it from settling.

- One of the messiest jobs is cleaning the chimney. If it can be done by a professional before you arrive, all the better. However, you can clean it yourself (see pages 82–83). Do it early in your cleaning.

- Remove things such as picture hooks, window shade hooks, and old curtain rods, and fill holes with spackle or putty. Also throw out any junk in the attic, basement, or garage.

- Start from the top down, the top being the attic. In the rooms, clean light fixtures, sweep or vacuum walls, window frames, and floor moldings first. Do floors last.

- Check the light-bulb situation and make a list of what you need. You want to be able to have the house properly illuminated your first night there.

- Check how well the sink drains flow. If the traps have a plug, now is an excellent time to clean them (see pages 160–61).

- Give the bathrooms a good cleaning. Scrub down showers and tubs, clean both toilet bowls and toilet tanks (see page 82). Make sure the grout around the tub and shower edges is in good shape. If not, repair before anyone bathes (see pages 104–7).

- Clean windows. If it's winter and storm windows are up, put this job off until the storm windows come down in the spring unless the windows are really grimy.

- Give the kitchen stove and refrigerator a going-over. Don't neglect the oven, the broiler, and the burners on the stove. Vacuum the condenser coils on the back of the fridge, defrost, and make sure the interior and the drip pan underneath are not forgotten.

- Give cabinets and closets a thorough cleaning. Line shelving with shelf paper.

- After thoroughly cleaning and vacuuming the interior, shampoo any carpets and wax the floors.

- Sweep patios, porches, garages, and other exterior spaces.

- Spread newspapers over areas that will be heavily trafficked by movers.

Household Cleaners and Polishes—Poisons in Your Home

Many consumers tend to think anything sold must be safe. However, over forty thousand people poisoned by household cleaners and polishes received emergency room treatment in 1982. Of these poisonings, 90 percent involved children under five years old. Cleaners and polishes are effective because they contain strong toxic chemicals. Even aerosol disinfectants, air fresheners, and deodorizers contain not only aerosol propellant chemicals but also strong chemicals whose long-term health effects are suspected of being potentially harmful.

• When using household chemical products or different brands of one type of product, don't mix them. Adverse chemical reactions may occur, for example, when different brands of drain openers are mixed, or if ammonia is mixed with bleach. The labels list precautions and proper poison treatment; don't remove them.

• Avoid breathing cleaner and polish fumes and avoid skin and eye contact. Use protective clothing and gloves.

• Literally every cleaning job in the house, as well as most maintenance chores, can be performed by using cheap, common household chemicals or goods such as ammonia, vinegar, and club soda. Many of the helpful-hints books on the market list them. Check these out.

BASIC HOUSEWARES

Besides the initially required cleaning equipment listed on page 49 and the basic tools listed in the next section, there are housewares and supplies that come in handy when you least expect them. You should have the following on hand:

— A good first-aid kit
— A portable radio
— A flashlight
— Batteries
— Candles or a kerosene lamp (and kerosene)
— Light bulbs
— Matches
— Assorted screws/nails/wall anchors/fasteners/picture hooks (it's always a good idea to pick up extra when you buy items for a specific job)
— Steel wool
— Sandpaper: various grits
— Mat knife and/or razor blades
— Scissors
— String

— Tape: masking, cellophane, and a strong duct or strapping tape
— Lubricants such as spray WD-40 (with nozzle) or 3-in-1
— Glues: both a white liquid glue such as Elmer's and a household cement or epoxy
— A drain opener (we recommend liquid; see page 160)
— An insecticide
— Rags and dust or polishing cloths
— Extra fuses/vacuum cleaner bags/heater and air-conditioning and heating system filters (unless your present filters can be cleaned and reused)
— Extension cords
— Furniture polish
— Floor wax
— Standard all-purpose household cleaners (especially ammonia)

THE EIGHT ESSENTIAL TOOLS AND HOW TO USE THEM

No matter how unhandy you consider yourself, you are going to need certain tools right away. After all, you can't call in a professional to hang a picture, tighten a loose screw on a shutter hinge, or assemble that prefab record cabinet you just picked up on sale. An objective look at many household fix-it chores will prove them to be totally within your capability. (For a listing of the easiest chores and how to do them, see Chapter 7: *"The VHH* Repair and Maintenance Guide.")

Buy high-quality tools. Cheap tools can actually be uneconomical, and even dangerous. A cheap ladder can collapse, a poorly forged screwdriver can shatter under pressure, and cheap drill bits dull so easily they can't penetrate harder woods and can burn up a power drill (whereas carbide-tipped drill bits perform better, last longer, and can be resharpened). You usually get just what you pay for, and a bargain usually is not a bargain.

Hammer

A medium-weight twelve- to thirteen-ounce curved claw hammer is good for general purposes. (The ounces refer to the weight of the head. Tack hammers weigh seven ounces; professional carpenters' hammers, sixteen to twenty ounces.)

- Hold a hammer near the end of the handle and use a free-swinging motion that comes from the shoulder and elbow. To start a nail, hold it in place and tap it gently a few times until it is firmly set. Hit it straight in, keeping your eye on the nail. (See fig. 4-1.)

Fig. 4–1

- To avoid hammer marks on wood, use a nail set (see fig. 4-2) or another nail to sink the head of a nail at least one-eighth inch into the wood.

Fig. 4–2

- To remove a nail, use the claw end of the hammer. Place a small block of wood under the head of the hammer to avoid marking the wood (see fig. 4-3).

Fig. 4–3

Screwdrivers
You need two types of screwdrivers for household repairs—straight-blade (see fig. 4-4) and Phillips (see fig. 4-5). Both come in various sizes. The blade of the screwdriver should fit the slot in the screw (see fig. 4-6).

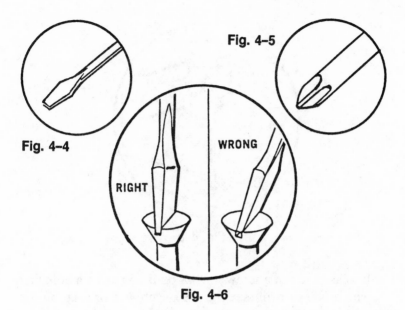

Fig. 4–5

Fig. 4–4

RIGHT

WRONG

Fig. 4–6

An alternative to buying several screwdrivers is to buy one combination spiral-ratchet screwdriver (see fig. 4-7), which usually comes with interchangeable tips (screwdrivers as well as drill bits that usually are stored in the handle). Pushing down on the handle causes the head of a ratchet screwdriver to turn and either drives a screw or drills a hole, depending on the tip you use.

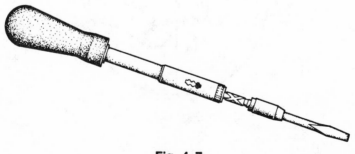

Fig. 4–7

• When using a screwdriver, push against the head of the screw as you turn it (see fig. 4-8).

Fig. 4–8

- It's easier to put a screw into wood if you make a hole first with a nail or drill (see fig. 4-9). Rub wax or soap on the screw to make it go in even easier.

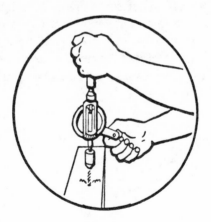

Fig. 4–9

Pliers

A slip-joint pliers (see fig. 4-10) can be used for endless jobs around the house. The slip joint is located at the pivot and allows the pliers to be set for either a normal or a wider opening. Don't scrimp—buy a pair made from forged steel. They should measure about eight inches in length.

Fig. 4–10

- The farther back on the handles you hold the pliers, the better leverage you get.
- Use pliers to hold a nut while you turn a bolt with a screwdriver (see fig. 4-11).

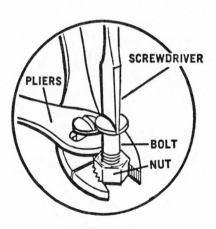

Fig. 4–11

- Use pliers to remove nails or brads (small, headless tacks). Pull the nail out at the same angle it was driven in. Use small blocks under the pliers if you need leverage (see fig. 4-12).

Fig. 4–12

- Use pliers to bend or cut wire or to straighten a bent nail (see fig. 4-13).

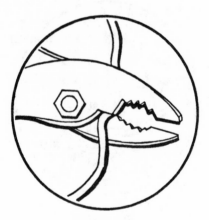

Fig. 4–13

- Use pliers to turn nuts. Wrap tape or cloth around the nut to avoid scratching it or put some adhesive tape on the face of the jaws (see fig. 4-14).

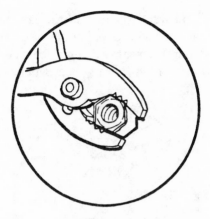

Fig. 4–14

Handsaw

A handsaw (see fig. 4-15) with about ten teeth to the inch (see fig. 4-16) is good for most household work. Store in a dry place; saws can rust.

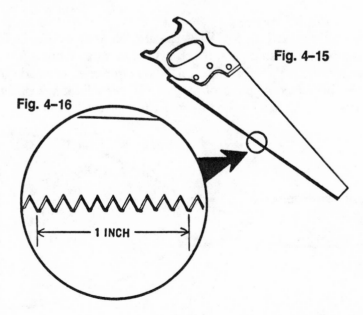

Fig. 4–15

Fig. 4–16

1 INCH

- Mark where you want to cut. Pull the saw back and forth several times to start a groove. Let the weight of the saw do the cutting at first. If you are sawing a board, it will be easier if you support and hold it firmly near where you're cutting (see fig. 4-17).

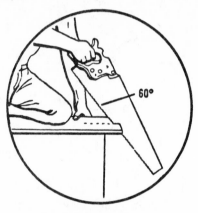

60°

Fig. 4–17

Wall Scraper

A wall scraper (see fig. 4-18) can also serve as a putty knife and plaster or spackle applicator. One that has about a four-inch blade is the most practical. The better ones are made of one fairly flexible piece of tough steel, with the shank of the handle being sandwiched between two pieces of wood.

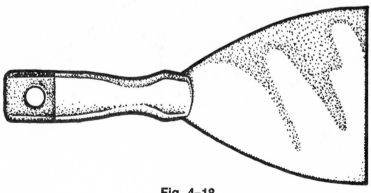

Fig. 4–18

Tape Measure
A tape measure has a thousand uses around the house. The best ones are a flexible steel tape in a case with a rewind mechanism. Buy one at least twelve feet long.

Flashlight
Not only useful if the lights go out, a flashlight is also handy for attic, basement, closets, cabinets, in the crawl space under the house, and outside at night. Though *The VHH* recommends rechargeable batteries for radios, cassette recorders, children's games, and the like, flashlights should be equipped with good alkaline batteries, which don't lose their charge over time.

Plunger
Also called the "plumber's friend," a plunger (see fig. 4-19; also see page 160) is used to loosen either material clogging sink drains and toilets or minor obstructions in the main drain line. Some have cones extending beyond the normal cup, and though they do exert a greater force, they may not always work on sinks because of their shape. The important thing is to make sure the one you buy works for both sinks and toilets.

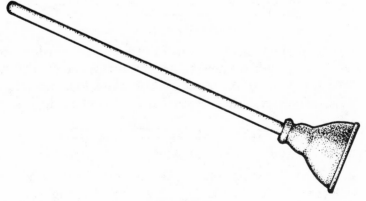

Fig. 4–19

- Place the plunger over the clogged drain and press down on the handle repeatedly. This sends a high-pressure ram of water against the obstruction, often dislodging it. Make sure the overflow hole of the sink, lavatory, or tub is blocked with a wet washrag to ensure that the plunger exerts the proper pressure.

- If a sink trap that is clogged has a screw-out plug, remove the plug and clean out the trap. A plunger can possibly force the obstruction farther into the main drain line, where it can cause even more trouble.

NAILS, SCREWS, AND BOLTS

The VHH recommends buying these at hardware stores that let you get as many or as few as you want. Too often they are prepackaged in amounts that force you to purchase more than you need or want.

Nails

- Nails, the most useful fasteners about the house, come in two shapes.
  — Box nails (see fig. 4-20) have large heads. Use them for rough work when appearance doesn't matter.

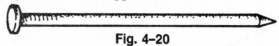

Fig. 4–20

  — Finishing nails (see fig. 4-21) have very small heads. You can drive them below the surface and cover them with putty or plastic wood. Use where looks are important, as in putting up paneling or building shelves.

Fig. 4–21

- The size and weight of most nails are expressed by the term "penny," expressed as "d." Here are the lengths of the more common size nails:

2 d	1″
3 d	1¼″
4 d	1½″
5 d	1¾″
6 d	2″
8 d	2½″
10 d	3″
12 d	3¼″
16 d	3½″
20 d	4″

Screws and Bolts

- Use screws where holding power is important. Also, if necessary, they can be installed and removed without damage to a surface. Use them to install towel bars and curtain rods, to repair drawers, to mount hinges, and lots more.

- Wood screws are available in round head (see fig. 4-22) and flat head (see fig. 4-23). Flat heads recess, round do not.

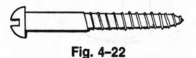

Fig. 4–22

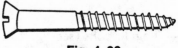

Fig. 4–23

- Where screws work loose, you can refill the holes with matchsticks or wood putty and replace them.

- To attach screws securely to walls, use molly bolts, toggle bolts, or plastic anchor screws. Molly and toggle bolts are both used for attaching things to hollow surfaces such as plaster or sheetrock walls. Anchor screws expand to grip a solid wall.
  — Molly bolts (see fig. 4-24) have two parts. To install, first make a small hole in the plaster and drive the casing in even with the wall surface. Tighten the screw to spread the casing in the back. Remove the screw and put it through the item you are hanging, into the casing, and tighten.

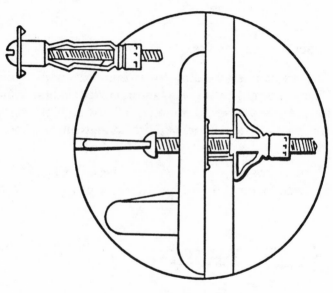

Fig. 4–24

  — Toggle bolts (see fig. 4-25). Drill a hole in the plaster large enough for the folded toggle to go through. Remove the toggle. Put the bolt through the towel bar or whatever you are hanging. Replace the toggle. Push the toggle through the wall and tighten with a screwdriver.

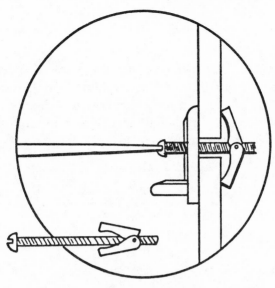

Fig. 4-25

— Plastic anchor screws (see fig. 4-26). To install, first
make a small hole in the wall and drive the casing in
even with the wall surface. Put the screw through the
item and into the casing and tighten.

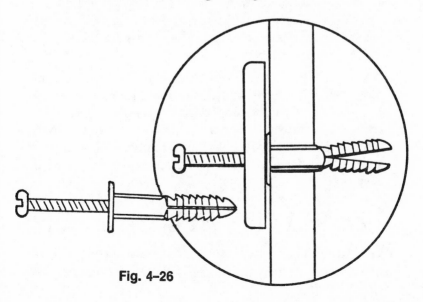

Fig. 4-26

LUMBER

- Lumber comes in certain standard sizes. What it's called and what you get are two different things. Take this into consideration if you're putting in bookcases, adding to the closet shelving situation, or building even more ambitious projects where you need to measure to the inch.

If You Order	You Get
1" × 2"	¾" × 1⅝"
1" × 3"	¾" × 2⅝"
1" × 4"	¾" × 3⅝"
1" × 5"	¾" × 4⅝"
1" × 6"	¾" × 5⅝"
1" × 8"	¾" × 7⅝"
1" × 10"	¾" × 9⅝"
1" × 12"	¾" × 11½"

- If you need a board thicker than ¾ inch, you must order a "five quarter" board, which should be 1¼ inches thick but actually measures $1\frac{1}{16}$ inches. The widths are the same as in the preceding table.

- Boards are divided into two basic grades: select and common. Select has fewer knots and should be used when appearance is of prime importance. Compare. Sometimes common grade can be of high quality; it varies. Always select the lumber yourself. Many lumberyards throw in warped and damaged pieces with orders, especially when they deliver.

CHECKING OUT THE BASIC SYSTEMS

Your first few months as a virgin homeowner are predominantly a time of getting acquainted. Two chapters in this book are especially important at this time. They are Chapter 6: *The VHH* Timetable" and Chapter 8: "Around the House: How Everything Works and How You Can Make It Work More Efficiently."

Whatever month you move in, do everything recommended in that month's timetable. Then when you've been in the house a year, you will have completed a full cycle of maintenance.

However, there are a few checks you should take care of as you're settling in. These shouldn't wait until *The VHH-* recommended month rolls around.

- Make an appointment to have the heating system checked for safety and efficiency (see pages 165–74). The system should be cranked up and tested out. You don't want winter to catch you unprepared.

- Check out the fans and air conditioning (see page 81 and pages 174–76). Have them serviced if they don't function properly.

- If you arrive in midwinter or midsummer, make sure the filters on the air-conditioning unit or the furnace are cleaned or replaced.

- Drain the hot-water heater (see page 78).

- Check the metal roof flashing (see page 78 and pages 190–91).

- Check roof gutters and rain spouts during a rain (see pages 142–48).

- Set up a house file (see page 78).

Chapter 5

GETTING TO KNOW THE TERRITORY

If, in addition to settling into your first home, you are relocating to a new area, you have the added task of getting to know the territory. Though you've already made a rough evaluation of the neighborhood and community before buying your house, now you have to get down to specifics. After all, you are making a new beginning—in your first house in a new place.

The three rules of thumb here are to be observant, be inquisitive, and be friendly. Even a postcard rack in a drugstore might have cards of local sights you didn't know about. And the lady you started talking to in the supermarket might turn out to be your new best friend. It's the unexpected (and they'll be plenty of it) that can make life agreeable. What makes a community a desirable place to live, to raise a family, to work, and to retire is the quality of human relations.

CHECKLIST

Here are some of the things you'll have to do to establish yourself in a new neighborhood. A bit of this overlaps with our recommendations in *"The VHH* Moving Timetable" in Chapter 3.

- Find out emergency numbers and locations of hospitals, fire-alarm boxes, and police station.
- Introduce yourself and your family to your new neighbors.
- At a later date, when you get to know them better, leave an extra set of house and car keys with your favorite neighbors.
- Enroll the kids in school. Transfer their school records.
- Find your new doctor, dentist, mechanic, and veterinarian. Transfer the records.
- Get a *detailed* map of the area.
- Open a new bank account.
- Arrange garbage pickup and deliveries of newspapers, mail, milk, etc.
- Start getting to know local merchants. Open charge accounts.
- Fill out check-cashing applications at supermarkets and other stores.
- Visit or join local civic organizations, religious groups, neighborhood associations, Scout troops, etc.
- Apply for a card at the local library.
- Change your voting registration.
- Check on local transportation.
- Start scouting around for baby-sitters.
- Give your friends your new address and phone number.
- Do you want to have a housewarming?

SOURCES OF INFORMATION

Three Main Sources

Practically everything you need to learn the ropes can be obtained from the following three sources:

- Neighbors and other locals. Combine getting information with making new friends. Use specific questions to introduce yourself; the rest will take care of itself. Also, just as getting a second doctor's or second repairperson's opinion is essential, get second opinions about the community from your new acquaintances. It's interesting to compare them; these second opinions can give you additional insight into your community.

- A good map. Your knowledge of the terrain can be greatly enhanced by getting the most detailed area map available and using it daily. When you get in the car to go anywhere, consult the map for alternate ways to get there and try to memorize street names as you drive. This form of exploration will inform you of the lay of the land, and you'll discover things like a municipal swimming pool, a day-care center, or a community garden you may want to become part of. What you don't think to ask the neighbors about might appear around a corner.

- The local newspaper. Here you'll get the goings-on in town —what local government and civic organizations are up to; information on exhibits, theaters, movies, concerts; things for sale; even who's getting married, divorced, and picked up for speeding (which can inform you that there's either a speed trap or an active police force). In short, a local newspaper can provide the clearest picture of what makes your town tick.

Other Sources

- The Welcome Wagon, if it's efficient, should visit within a week or two after you move in. They usually furnish you with a directory of local businesses and discount coupons to use for shopping and getting introduced to these businesses. Invite them in and ask questions; they can be a great help.

- The Chamber of Commerce also can provide information about local businesses and perform special services such as arranging informative tours of local industries and giving you information on any sights of interest in the vicinity.
- The Yellow Pages of the telephone directory will show you the variety of goods and services available in both the community and the general area.

WHAT YOU SHOULD EXPECT FROM YOUR COMMUNITY

What Your Local Tax Money Should Provide

- an education for your children from kindergarten through at least grade 12
- cultural programs
- medical care
- acceptable transportation and public utilities
- good police and fire protection

Schools and How to Evaluate Them

School costs usually are a community's biggest budget item. You can judge the quality of local schools as follows:

- talking with schoolteachers or other parents
- asking to sit in on classes and noting teacher-student relationships and how creative or stimulating the classroom atmosphere is
- examining how much money is spent per pupil and comparing this figure to state and national averages
- checking achievement test ratings and comparing them with state and national averages

- looking for special services and facilities such as science and language laboratories, libraries, and psychiatric and counseling services
- attending Parent Teacher Association meetings. If your children are enrolled in the school, it is best to involve yourself with the PTA at least until you have informed yourself enough about the school system to be assured that the educational needs of your children are being met.

Adult Programs and Night School

One of the most overlooked resources of the local school system is its evening program. Mostly free of charge, it may offer everything from home economics, sewing, and stenography to woodworking, word processing, and French. It's a perfect way to make yourself more handy or fill in the gaps in your education.

Libraries

A good library can be an important influence in a community. Aside from its supply of books, periodicals, pamphlets, documents, and audiovisual reference materials, a library with adequate personnel and resources may sponsor programs such as film forums, music listening groups, discussion programs for adults, and story hours for children. If a smaller community doesn't have a library, often state library commissions and regional bookmobiles provide helpful services and resources. Check these out.

Community Health Services

Don't overlook the wide variety of community health services available. They can save you a considerable amount of money by providing a wide range of services from immunizations and prenatal, dental, and dermatological care to treatment of mental disorders and diseases like diabetes.

Health Maintenance Organizations

A viable alternative to costly health and hospitalization insurance can be a local HMO. These are organizations of doctors, hospitals, and others offering enrolling members who pay a monthly or quarterly fee a wide range of health services, including surgery and extended hospital care in case of emergency or illness. HMO's have family plans, and the emphasis is on early detection through regular testing and checkups.

National Organizations
The following agencies are found in most communities. The address of the national organization is given below. If you cannot find the agency in your local phone book, you can write for the chapter or location nearest you. This list will also give you an idea of the wealth of services and organizations available.

American Association of Credit Counselors
1111 S. Woodward
Royal Oak, MI 48067

Affiliate agencies provide help in budgeting and credit planning. Some services free or at reduced fees.

American Association of Marriage and Family Counselors
225 Yale Ave.
Claremont, CA 91711

Help in locating family counselors and other services.

Big Brothers/Big Sisters of America
117 S. 17th St.
Philadelphia, PA 19103

Can provide trained volunteers to work with boys and girls.

Boys' Clubs of America
771 First Ave.
New York, NY 10017

Can provide activities for children.

Boy Scouts of America
North Brunswick, NJ 08902

Can provide activities for children and teenagers.

Closer Look
1201 16th St., N.W.
Washington, DC 20036

Helps handicapped children and their families.

Family Planning and Information Services 300 Park Ave. S. New York, NY 10010	Will provide information on birth control, abortion, and fertility problems.
Family Service Association of America 44 E. 23rd St. New York, NY 10010	Help in locating appropriate services for counseling and therapy.
Girls' Clubs of America 205 Lexington Ave. New York, NY 10016	Can provide activities for children.
Girl Scouts of the U.S.A. 830 Third Ave. New York, NY 10022	Can provide activities for children and teenagers.
North American Council on Adoptable Children 250 E. Blaine Riverside, CA 92507	Can help adoptive or potential adoptive parents.
Parents Anonymous 2810 Artesid Blvd. Redondo Beach, CA 90278	Provides help to parents who are afraid they are abusing or might abuse their children.
Parents Without Partners 7910 Woodmont Ave. Washington, DC 20014	Provides educational and support meetings and family activities.

Government Agencies

The following agencies are part of local, state, or federal government. Look in the phone book under the name of your municipality, county, or state.

- Invaluable free advice and information on close-to-home matters from gardens to garbage: Extension Service of the U.S. Department of Agriculture (see pages 215–16)

- General assistance in obtaining resources and financial as-

sistance: Department of Public Welfare, Department of Social Services, Department of Human Resources
- Help with housing problems: Public Housing Authority, Department of Housing and Urban Development
- For legal help: Friend of the Court, Legal Aid

More to Look For

- Learn the whereabouts of parks, playgrounds, swimming pools, and other facilities.
- Check to see if a local block association or crime watch group exists. Both of these hold regular meetings that will give you quick and easy entry into local circles.
- Voluntary associations such as art societies, community choruses, book review clubs, discussion groups, and community theater associations can all help to create an atmosphere conducive to development and use of cultural resources.
- Last but not least, local churches will offer you help in getting settled and oriented.

Chapter 6

THE VHH
TIMETABLE

January Through December

No house can stand alone. It needs help. Your help! The old adage "You take care of it, it takes care of you" applies to home maintenance.

Taking a house for granted means that you'll notice problems only when they're serious and costly to repair. Staying on top of the situation means less time for you and staying out of trouble in the long run. Just a few hours a month—not a lot to ask—can make that roof over your head last longer and provide you with lawn, shrubs, trees, and gardens you'll be proud of.

Here is one of the most valuable sections in *The VHH*. This calendar was created by researching, by talking with other homeowners, and by keeping detailed records of what needed doing when. Homeowners living in more temperate climates will have an easier go of it, but we've covered all bases here —and from Palm Springs to Bangor, homeowners can pick and choose what's applicable to them.

JANUARY

- Check furnace filters. They take quite a beating this time of year. Either clean or replace them (see page 169).

- If you cut your own firewood, now is the time to do it, cold as it may be. Dormant trees have less sap, and if you cut

76

now, wood will season well and be ready for burning in autumn.

- Mark your electric circuits (see pages 155–57). A chart or labels in or near your fuse or circuit-breaker box should show exactly what each circuit involves and what amperage fuse is required. Do this by turning on everything in the house, then unscrewing one fuse or breaking one circuit at a time and marking what goes off. The more people involved in this operation, the quicker it will go. Also, for those with fuse boxes, at this time check your supply of fuses. You never want to be caught short, and you *never* want to switch amperages.

- Write for garden catalogs (see pages 217–18 for a listing). Now is the time to plan for a garden or any trees or shrubs you want to plant.

FEBRUARY

- Check attic for condensation or—if you're living in a hard-winter zone—ice. Finding it can mean that the R value of your insulation isn't high enough, that the attic isn't properly ventilated, or that ice dams have formed on the roof eaves and snow melting behind them is seeping into the attic (see below).

- Check outside on a very gray, sunless winter day after a snow and look at the exterior of the house. Is snow melting on the roof or on the ground and shrubs around the house? If so, heat is escaping and you're insulation-deficient. Check the roof eaves for ice dams. These can wreak havoc with a roof, and the conditions that cause them must be corrected (see pages 189–90).

- Shake heavy, wet snow off the branches of your trees and shrubs as soon as possible after it has fallen. Its weight can break branches.

- While you're still outside, take a soil sample. Soil in its natural state is rarely fertile enough for best plant growth. A soil test is the only way to know what your turf needs. Your local U.S. Department of Agriculture Cooperative Extension Service will do a free analysis, and they'll do it faster in February (see pages 215–16).

- Paint or touch up radiators. Painting them while they're moderately warm makes the finish last longer. The heat tends to bake the paint on.

- Set up a house file. Include all documents and manuals you obtained from the previous owner (see pages 12–14) as well as invoices, receipts, instruction books, warranties, and any other material you are now accumulating that relates to your house and the appliances in it. An accordion file will accommodate all this if you don't have a file cabinet, and the file can be passed on to the next owner of the house if you ever move. Having readily accessible home documents and records can make life much easier, especially around tax time. If you already have a house file, a cold February day is the time to update it.

March

- Drain the hot-water heater. Near the bottom is a small tap. By draining a few quarts of water you remove scale, sediment, rust, and mineral (lime) deposits that settle on the bottom and reduce heat transfer. You should do this every few months, depending on how much sediment you find. If you have a home humidifier, drain collected sediment from it as well.

- Check metal (usually sheet copper or aluminum) roof flashing around chimneys, vent pipes, dormers, and at junctures of different roof angles to see if it's adequate to protect you from the April showers you're in store for. (For more about roof flashing, see pages 190–91.)

- Check out your lawn mower and garden tools. The greening of America is at hand. Clean the lawn mower of any accumulated grass (which you should have done when you stored it last fall), and wipe down the surface with a coat of light oil. Check the instruction book about checking the oil, changing spark plugs, etc. Also, with a flat file, sharpen the blades, and while you've got the file out, sharpen spades, shovels, hoes, and any other edged garden tools you might own. Tape any cracked handles, and give them a general cleaning up. (For more about mowing, see pages 206–8.)

- Saw off broken branches on trees and shrubs, and prune. Before new growth starts you can work with them more easily. Cutting away dead and excess branches makes for a healthier plant and more new foliage.

- Plant ground covers—they can be a better choice than grass in parts of the yard. Getting them into the ground in early spring gives them the chance to become well established before winter sets in (see pages 210–11).

- Take the time to put up stakes or other guards to protect young shrubs or trees from being run over by the lawn mower during the mowing season.

- Get your outdoor furniture ready for spring and summer. Remove any rust and corrosion from iron and aluminum furniture. Replace any canvas, fix up any furniture that broke last season.

APRIL

- Check roof gutters and downspouts during a rain to make sure they aren't clogged or leaking. Also check to see if rainwater is flowing away from the house (see pages 142–48).

- Before you remove storm windows and put up screens, set aside time to repair any screens that need it (see pages 131–33 for how to). Also give them a good brushing and wash them with detergent water either now or right before you install them.

- Turn on water to outside faucets. Check water hoses for leaks and get nozzles and sprinklers ready for service. Everything from pinholes to major breaks in a water hose can be mended. On your sprinklers make sure deposits haven't stopped up holes, and clean off rust with steel wool.

- Retension or replace window shades that need it. Shades work extremely well in both winter and summer in regulating room temperature. They close out sunlight in summer, let it in in winter.

- Check roof gutters and rain spouts during a rain. Are the gutters unclogged and is water flowing away from the house? Clogged gutters can cause serious rot and water damage, and poor drainage around the house can result in wet basements. (For how to clean and repair gutters, see pages 142–48.)

- Inspect trees for large broken branches that could fall and cause damage. Arbor Day is in April, and it's never a bad idea to plant a tree.

- April is a good month to start a compost pit, a great source of cheap fertilizer. (See page 210 for how to start one and pages 209–10 for fertilizer information.

MAY

- Check both the interior and the exterior of the house for needed painting and touch-ups and take care of it. Don't overlook trellises, doghouses, flower boxes, gates, fences, and the like. (See painting section, pages 90–100.)

- Masonry patrol time. Winter wreaks havoc on bricks or foundations of houses as well as on any retaining walls, walkways, and driveways. Inside, examine the cellar walls and floor for damp areas and any new cracks. Repair them. (See pages 137–42 for how to.)

- Test the air conditioning and fans in the attic and elsewhere. Clean or replace air-conditioning filters. Clean and oil fans. (There is a section on air-conditioner maintenance on pages 174–76.)

- Replace storm windows with screens except on windows of the air-conditioned rooms. The storm windows help keep the cool air in.

- Replace broken or badly cracked window panes, including storm window glass. (For how to do this, see pages 127–31.)

- Rugs need a break. They can lend a coziness and warmth to a house in winter. When spring has arrived, give them a thorough cleaning and sunning. Consider retiring them until the fall. If that doesn't appeal, at least reverse them or give them an alternate location if they're getting too much wear and tear.

- Houseplants can go outside now, especially if you'd like a break from each other. Some of them can be sunk in the ground, pot and all, if you wish to bring them indoors again or move them later.

- Get the swimming pool ready (if you've got one).

JUNE

- Be on the look out for swarming flights of insects, and examine house foundations for mud tubes that indicate termite infestation (see pages 194–95). Also watch for other pests.

- Time for the septic tank's annual inspection. Remove the cover (or cap) and measure the depth of sludge with a stick. If it's more than half full, have the tank pumped out. (More about septic tanks on pages 164–65.)

- The strong summer sun offers a perfect opportunity to air mattresses, pillows, and bedding. A mattress should also be vacuumed and turned, flipping it over one time and reversing head and foot the next.

JULY

- Check the crawl space under the house for rot and decay. If you find any, you should either increase ventilation under the house or blanket the ground with a vapor-resistant cover. (For specifics, see pages 191–95.)

- Clean flush-toilet tanks. Americans tend to be bowl-conscious because of national advertising, but the flush tank is where mineral deposits really build up and over time can hamper operation. Check the inner surface of the toilet bowl for any leaks into it; dry thoroughly, then see if tissue picks up water. If so, clean the flush system of slime and any other buildup. (For how a toilet works, see pages 161–62).

- Clean the filter of the kitchen exhaust fan. This should be done several times a year. These filters are real grease collectors. A hot July day, when grease is more easily removed, is also perfect for cleaning the motor and fan assembly. If you don't keep this fan and filter clean, you'll be replacing it pronto.

- Clean your air-conditioning filters and keep them clean. Check them out every few weeks. On the outside the finned surfaces of the condenser should be kept clean and free of leaves, mud, spider webs, etc. Shrubbery should also be cut back so as not to impede the flow of air. Lubricate your air conditioner according to instructions. This attention will make a difference in your electricity bill as well as in how long your air conditioner lasts. (See page 175.)

AUGUST

- If your fireplace is used frequently in the winter, check the chimney. Open the damper. With a flashlight look up to see if it is clogged or dirty. You can clean it yourself with a tire chain tied to a rope that you drag up and down the chimney. (Make sure the fireplace opening to the room is sealed with a sheet of plastic beforehand.) As a final step, remove soot and ash accumulations from the fireplace bed and use as fertilizer. Don't neglect to oil the damper, and make sure it fits tightly when closed. (See pages 184–87 for more about fireplaces.)

- Patch and seal the roof. It may be hot work, but liquid coatings and cements are more easily applied in high temperatures. And while you're up there, check flashing around chimneys, vent pipes, skylights, etc. (See pages 190–91.)

- Make sure all your doors have stops and guards. Doors that are constantly knocked against walls and moldings age a house unnecessarily. And any outside doors that occasionally get a kick to assist in opening should be equipped with kickplates across the bottom. (Also sand the edge of the door to prevent the sticking in the first place.) At this time repair any wall damage that might have been done. (For how to fix problem doors, see pages 124–27.)

- Clean out plumbing traps before they clog up entirely. Good-quality U traps have a plug in the bottom that can be unscrewed to allow the removal of gunk. Consider outfitting drains with strainers to catch debris that otherwise might clog drains. Note: Chemical drain cleaners (especially dry lye), if not used properly, can further clog a drain.

- Make an appointment to have the heating system checked for safety and efficiency. If necessary, have it cleaned and adjusted. (See pages 165–74.)

SEPTEMBER

- While you're having your heating system checked, now is the time either to replace or to clean thoroughly your thermostat. You might consider moving it to a location where it can be more sensitive to your heating needs, or replacing it with one that has a timer that automatically turns down the furnace at night or when you're away from the house. (See page 177.)

- If you use replacement furnace filters, make sure you're stocked up for the winter. In the average home, Fiberglas throwaway filters need replacing at least three times a year. Consider cleanable filters, and clean them monthly.

- Repair or replace broken or missing caulking and weather-stripping around doors, windows, and foundation walls. Proper sealing will prevent moisture damage from winter wind-driven rain or snow. Don't overlook the garage door. As well as weatherstripping along the sides, you can nail a strip of old carpet to the bottom to keep dirt and leaves from blowing under when it's closed. (See pages 134–37.)

- Do any necessary repainting. A warm September day is perfect for it. The south side of the house, which has been exposed to the most sunlight, is a good indicator of whether painting is necessary. (See painting section, pages 90–100.)

OCTOBER

- After Indian summer, remove air conditioners from windows, clean or replace filters, give the unit a going-over with the vacuum cleaner, cover, and store. If it cannot be removed from the window, clean and cover the exterior portion (buy or make a cover). (See page 175.)

- Install storm windows (unless you left them up on windows of air-conditioned rooms). Make sure they are sealed or are tight enough to keep cold air out. Also take the time to check window putty and replace any missing sections with new glazing compound.

- Clean and store all outdoor furniture, barbecue grills, gardening tools, and lawn mowers (check instructions for proper storage). Drain and clean fountains and pools (if you've got them). Note: you may want to leave the lawn mower out a bit longer if your grass is still growing or you want to run it over the yard to shred autumn leaves.

- Drain hoses of water and store. Drain outside faucets (sill cocks) and pipes to prevent freeze damage.
- Is your snow removal equipment ready to use? If you have a snow thrower, crank it up. Henceforth whenever you finish using it, oil all friction points and clean and dry it. And what about your snow shovel situation? Can the one or ones you have be pressed into service for another season? If you feel you ought to purchase a new one, consider one that's Teflon-coated. The coating makes the shoveling easier.
- If winter freezing and thawing ravage your concrete drive and walkways, think about protecting them with an anti-spalling compound. After repairs are made (see pages 139–42 for how to), brush, roll, or spray the compound on dry concrete and it will seal with a tough membrane.
- The clothes drier vent must be disassembled and cleaned of any lint buildup. This is a good time to install a heat saver that vents the heat and humidity (minus lint) into the house, where it is needed.
- Order a live Christmas tree (if you wait too late you might not be able to get one). Pick up your live evergreen right before Christmas, take home and decorate, then plant after Christmas. It doesn't cost a lot more than a cut tree and, as it grows and enhances your property, it will serve as a nice Christmas souvenir. Dig a hole for it before the ground freezes, and fill with straw or leaves.

NOVEMBER

- Clear roof gutters and down spouts of autumn leaves. They could cause serious problems and water damage if you don't. (See pages 142–48.)
- Clean out the shower heads. Chances are you'll be pleased at the improvement. Unscrew the head and remove sediment and mineral deposits with a stiff brush or coarse needle. Do the same to your kitchen sink spray unit, and make sure the hose is unkinked and leak-free.

- Take the time to change washers and repack any leaking faucets. It takes very little time, saves water, and prevents drip stains on porcelain. (For how to, see pages 101–4.)

- Patch torn wallpaper and glue down any curling edges. You can indefinitely postpone rewallpapering a room. The secret to patching is tearing the edge of the patch instead of cutting it with scissors. It blends better.

- Protect any plants that need it with winter mulch. The proper time to add it is before the ground has frozen hard.

DECEMBER

- Midwinter is a prime time for power failures. You should have on hand a store of candles, a working flashlight, even a kerosene lamp. A fireplace can help with your heating and cooking needs, and so can a charcoal grill set up in the garage or in a well-ventilated area. Open the refrigerator as infrequently as possible; the same goes for the doors of the house.

- Give the refrigerator a thorough cleaning, inside and out. Vacuum the condenser coils on back and underneath—it makes your fridge more energy-efficient.

- Check electric cords. Look for visible breaks in the insulation covering, frayed fabric cord covering, and deteriorating plugs. Appliances, lamps and cords, and any other household items that need repairs are safety hazards. Fix them! (For how to, see pages 115–20.) Also check any cords in storage. They should be kept in a cool, dry place and be loosely wound and free of knots, kinks, and sharp bends.

Chapter 7

THE VHH *REPAIR AND MAINTENANCE GUIDE*

Doing it yourself can save time as well as money. Say you've got a dripping faucet. By the time you search out a plumber and set up an appointment, then plan your day around being home when he arrives, you could have changed the washers in several faucets yourself. But there are times when hiring someone to do the job is well worth it. It can be better to be at work earning the money to pay a roofer than to do a rush job yourself and risk hundreds of dollars of damage to your ceilings when the roof leaks. *The VHH* advocates lessening your dependence on repairpeople—cutting down but not quitting.

To decide whether or not you should make a repair or hire an expert, answer these questions:

- What is the extent of the repair?

- What are your actual or potential skills?

- How much time will it take?
- How important is the repair compared to your time?
- What will it cost you in materials and tools?
- Are reputable repairpeople available, and what are their prices?
- Are standard materials required, and are they readily available to you? Remember, the person you hire should be able to get parts at discount and pass some of those savings on to you—it's labor where they make their money.
- Will the repair require more materials than labor, or more labor than materials?
- How much will you save if you do the work yourself?

And take the following into consideration:

- Difficulty—a complicated job sometimes can be a bargain if you hire it out to an expert, considering all the trouble you might get yourself into.
- Your time—don't begin a repair unless you have the time to do it right.
- Ability—base your planning on your own abilities, not on those of your neighbors. Is there someone you can pay for advice if you become stumped?
- Getting bailed out—once you begin a repair and invest time and money, don't expect that a professional will come in and finish the job for substantially less than what would have originally been charged.
- Quality material—avoid the cost of repeating the same repair because you used faulty materials or procedures.

A well-built house that is properly maintained doesn't wear out quickly. The wood your house is built with should outlast you. Timbers three to thirteen centuries old in Japanese temples are structurally sound, and so are those in America's oldest house in St. Augustine, Florida, going on three centuries old. A small amount of attention can keep your home in tip-top shape. Here is a list of the doable home repair and maintenance jobs, with instructions and illustrations. If you opt for hiring someone to do the job, see "Choosing a Professional," pages 148–50.

PAINTING

Of all home improvements, painting probably is the most doable and produces the most dramatic change in a short period of time. Good results are guaranteed if these four cardinal rules are followed:

- Properly prepare the surface for painting. Even the best paint won't last on a poorly prepared surface.

- Read the paint container label. Choose the proper coating for the surface.

- Use good-quality paint. It protects longer and better. It takes the same amount of time to apply good-quality paint as it does a cheapo brand that won't last as long.

- Apply the paint correctly. Improper application can be as damaging as a poorly prepared surface.

To Paint or Not to Paint

There is a compulsion in this country to keep wood freshly painted. People feel it must be done (1) for appearance and (2) for protection of the surface. They are wrong on both counts. *Not* painting wood can enhance its appearance as well as make it last longer (especially if the paint traps moisture). Wood that is not sealed with paint will take on a soft luster and develop rich hues. New wood can be finished with wax or oil, especially tung oil, for a finished look that gradually acquires a lovely patina. Even outdoor wood doesn't necessarily require painting—weathered wood has a beauty all its own. (Leave a porch floor unpainted after you strip all the peeling paint off and see what we mean.)

In short, not painting wood—and some experts recommend

dispensing with paint altogether—has the advantage of saving money, time, and energy. *The VHH* suggests you try it and live with unfinished wood awhile, then decide. You can always paint over it.

Surface Preparation

Preparing a surface for paint should take the most time in any painting job. In general a surface to be painted should be firm, smooth, and clean. All holes in wallboard or plaster must be patched. See pages 112–15 for how to to this.

Washing a wall makes all the difference. Grease or grime must be absent for good paint adhesion. They can be removed from any surface except drywall with a detergent solution, ammoniated cleanser, or mineral spirits. Kitchen walls and ceilings usually are covered with a film of cooking grease that may extend to the walls and ceilings just outside the room entrance. Bathroom walls and ceilings may have excessive grime as well. For oil-base paint, the surface must also be completely dry; otherwise the paint will seal in the moisture. Latex or water-base paint can be applied to a damp but not wet surface. Check the paint-can label for additional or special instructions and follow them!

Paint Failure

Paint problems seldom are due to the paint. Here is a list of common paint failures and their causes:

Failure	Cause
blistering, peeling, or discoloration	excessive wetting of paint from behind or in front—moisture in the wood
crossgrain cracking	may be caused by too-frequent repainting with oil-base paint; the thick paint coating is too hard to stand constant expansion of wood and cracks

Failure	Cause
mildew	continuous warm and damp conditions
intercoat peeling	lack of adhesion between top- and undercoats; primer and topcoat of oil-base paint incompatible because of too long a delay between coats, or surface was too smooth, hard, glossy, or oily latex paint separates from heavily chalked surfaces
excessive chalking	poor-quality paint used, paint improperly applied, or thinned excessively

Paint Selection

Selection need not be too much of a problem. Simply define your needs. First consider whether you need an exterior paint (exposed to weather) or an interior paint. Then consider the surface you are painting: wood, metal, masonry, etc. Some all-purpose paints can be used on many surfaces; other paints are more specialized. Usually the more specialized, the better.

Next consider any special requirements. For example, old, chalky surfaces are generally not sound bases for latex or water-base paints. Nonchalking paint may be advisable where chalk rundown would discolor adjacent brick or stone surfaces. Perhaps mildew is a problem. If so, it should be removed and efforts made to correct its cause (excess moisture is the major culprit). Mildew-resistant paints are available for use where such problems occur. Basically, there are three kinds of paint:

- Latex or water-base rubber paint: the easiest to use because it can be washed off floors, brushes, rollers with plain water before it dries.

- Oil-base or solvent-thinned: These are very durable, highly resistant to staining and damage, can withstand frequent scrubbings, and give one-coat coverage. (Many latex paints are advertised as having similar properties.)
- Acrylic or plastic-base: Though more expensive, acrylics have long-lasting colors and are quite resistant to weather.

There are also three paint finishes:

- Glossy finishes look shiny and clean easily.
- Flat finishes reduce glare but more readily become dirty.
- Semigloss is in between and has properties of both glossy and flat.

Because enamel is durable and easy to clean, semigloss or full-gloss enamel is recommended for woodwork and for the walls of kitchens, bathrooms, and laundry rooms. For the walls of nurseries and playrooms, either oil-base or latex semigloss enamel is suggested. Flat paint works well on the walls of living rooms, dining rooms, and other nonwork or nonplay rooms.

Color Selection

- Light colors repel heat while dark tones absorb it.
- Light colors make a room seem larger, cooler, airier. Conversely, dark colors make an overly large room appear smaller, warmer, cozier.
- Ceilings appear higher when lighter than the walls and lower when darker than the walls. The darker ceiling color also camouflages flaws.
- If one side of a narrow hallway is painted with a dark shade of a color and the other side with a lighter shade of the same color, the effect is to make the hallway seem wider.
- Paint usually dries to a slightly different color or shade. For a fast preview of the final color, brush a sample swatch of the paint on a piece of clean, white blotting paper. The

paper will immediately absorb the wet gloss, and the color will be about that of the paint when it dries on the wall.

- Colors often change under artificial lighting. Look at color swatches both in daylight and under artificial lighting.

- The type of artificial lighting can also make a difference. For instance, incandescent lighting casts a warm, yellow glow. Fluorescent usually gives off a cooler, blue hue, unless a warm, white fluorescent tube is used.

- Most paint stores use fluorescent lighting, and consequently a color that seems to be one shade in the paint store may look different in your home. Adjacent colors also affect the appearance.

Estimating Quantity

For large jobs, paint usually is bought by the gallon. The average gallon of paint covers about five hundred square feet, which is the wall and ceiling area of a ten-foot-square, ten-foot-high room. If it's a second coat, the gallon should cover about nine hundred square feet. Usually the label indicates the number of square feet a gallon will cover when applied as directed. Have dimensions handy before you go paint shopping.

Keep track of how much paint or wallpaper was used when painting or wallpapering. Because light-switch plates usually are removed before painting, many homeowners make a note of it there. On the wall behind a picture will also do—anywhere as long as it's consistent from room to room so you won't have to search. Doing this will help avoid waste the next time you paint.

When to Paint

For best results with oil-base, latex, or acrylic paints and for an easier and better paint job, the weather conditions should be right.

- Paint when weather is mild and dry. The less humidity in the air, the quicker paint will dry.

- Low and high temperatures adversely affect paint. Freezing temperatures should be avoided with any paint. Oil-base paints have an even lower tolerance—never apply them when the temperature is below forty degrees Fahrenheit. Temperatures above ninety degrees Fahrenheit are not only torture to the painter but also may cause the paint to dry too quickly, causing brush lap marks to appear in a freshly painted surface. Consult the label for temperature limitations.

- Start outside painting after the morning dew has evaporated. Stop outside painting in late afternoon or early evening on cool fall days. This is far more important with latex paint than with oil-base paint, because condensation dilutes latex.

- Apply paint to surfaces after they have been exposed to sunlight and are in the shade. A good rule is to follow the sunlight around the house.

- Don't paint in windy or dusty weather or when insects may get caught in the paint. Insects usually are the biggest problem during fall evenings. Don't try to remove them from wet paint; brush them off after the paint dries.

Equipment

- Rollers: For speed and convenience, homeowners usually use rollers on walls, ceilings, and other large surfaces, then use a brush at corners, along edges, and in other places a roller cannot reach. Rollers also work well on masonry and metal surfaces. Proper depth of the pile or nap on roller covers is important and varies from one surface to another. Follow the manufacturer's recommendations.

- Brushes: Woodwork usually is painted with a brush, which will give better penetration on wood than either a roller or a can of spray paint. Different kinds of brushes and rollers are recommended for use with different kinds of paint. For example, natural-bristle brushes are best for applying oil-base paints, varnishes, lacquers, and other paints because the natural fibers resist the strong solvents found in those paints. The characteristics of bristle also affect how well paint is transferred to the painting surface.

- Other applicators: Rectangular applicators offer the speed and convenience of rollers. Like rollers, they are good for large surfaces, and they have the advantage of not speckling you with paint, as a roller can. Also on the market are specially shaped rollers and other applicators for painting woodwork, corners, edges, and other close places. Some may work fine, but a small brush is hard to beat.

Note: At the end of a job, take the extra time to thoroughly clean your brushes and rollers. They will last indefinitely. In the midst of a paint job, wet brushes and rollers can be wrapped tightly in plastic or cellophane wrap for overnight storage.

The Best Way to Paint
Painting is painting, but there are ways to do it more efficiently. Read on. It'll make a difference in how much paint you use, how long it takes to apply it, how it looks, and how long it lasts.

- Rooms
  — Preferably, remove all furnishing from a room to be painted. Otherwise, cover furniture, fixtures, and floor with drop cloths or newspapers. No matter how careful you are, there will always be some spill, drip, or splatter of paint.
  — If you don't wish to paint light-switch and wall-plug plates, remove them. (Guard against shock while doing so—don't stick the screwdriver in them.)
  — Paint ceilings first, walls next, and woodwork (including doors, windows, and trim) last.
  — As you begin a ceiling or a wall, paint a border along the edge and next to the moldings. This is called "cut-

ting in." Do it when applying both coats and avoid getting paint on the moldings. Start painting with the roller next to the painted cut-in strip, using steady, slow strokes. When using a roller, work in strips, always overlapping the wet edge of the previously painted strip.
— Excess paint should be removed from a roller by working it back and forth across the tray grid; otherwise a roller will sling paint if you work too fast.
• Woodwork
— Start with ceiling trim, then baseboards (using a cardboard masker as you paint), then windows, doors, and door frames—in that order.
— Flush doors can be painted with a roller. On paneled doors, some parts can be rollered.
• Windows

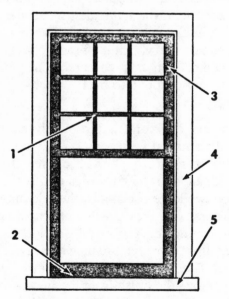

Fig. 7-1

— Paint windows in this order (see fig. 7-1): (1) mullions, (2) horizontal of sash, (3) verticals of sash, (4) verticals of frame, (5) horizontal frame and sill.

— After you paint and before the paint sets, move the sash up and down to prevent the window from drying shut.

— You can mask panes of window glass with any of the following:

1. wet newspaper—the moisture will paste it down and also prevent paint from soaking in.

2. a light layer of petroleum jelly such as Vaseline rubbed around the edges of the glass.

3. Masking tape and liquid masking—remove the tape when the paint is dry to the touch.

— An alternative to masking is to remove paint smeared on glass with a single-edged razor blade or other suitable scraper. Here's how: After the paint is set but before it hardens, cut a line through the paint with a utility knife or razor blade where the glass meets the wood. Then, starting at one corner, carefully scrape up a section of the paint and slowly lift it off the glass. If it breaks, peel up another section large enough to grasp with your fingers and continue to peel.

• Exterior
   — Make sure that paint is thoroughly mixed. Oil paint should be stirred frequently during use.
   — It's best to paint from a small bucket. If you are using several gallons, it's a good idea to mix it all together in one or two large containers, then decant it into sealed containers. This is especially important if color paint is used—paint colors can vary from one can to another.
   — Never dip the brush more than a third the length of the bristles. Then pat off excess paint to avoid dripping paint as you move the brush from the bucket to the surface.
   — Begin painting at the highest part of the house and work downward. This will avoid paint spilling or dripping on surfaces already painted.
   — Complete all broad main areas first, then go back and paint the trim.

— To avoid brush marks, always end up painting an area by brushing back into the area already painted.

— When painting circular objects such as downspouts, first apply the paint diagonally. Then paint across the diagonal strokes by working downward along the long dimension. (See fig. 7-2.)

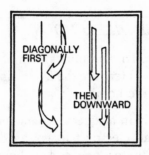

Fig. 7–2

Paint Storage

When paint is stored for an extended period, a skin often forms over the top. Here are some tips for preventing this:

• Store the can upside down (make sure it's tightly sealed).

• Before capping a can of oil paint, pour four tablespoons of mineral spirits on top or sprinkle it with paint thinner. Don't stir the paint until it's time to reuse it.

• Cut a circular disc of aluminum foil or waxed paper and slide it into the paint can over the paint. Press out the air bubbles and replace the lid tightly.

• Breathe—yes, breathe—into the can before sealing it. Moisture trapped in the can keeps a film from forming on the paint.

• Melted paraffin over the top seals paint best of all, as it does jellies.

• Store latex in a warm place. Freezing ruins latex.

- Paint a line on the outside of the can to mark the paint level. This tells you how much paint you have left as well as what color it is and saves your having to reopen the can to find out.
- If a film has formed on the surface, leave it until you use the paint. Cut along the edge with a knife, then remove it.

THE WELL-OILED HOUSE

A house has more friction points than you think, and these require lubrication. Here are the five main types of lubricants and their uses in the home.

- Light oil, usually in a squeeze container
  — Use on small electric fans (put a drop or two in the reservoir, if there is one, and on the fan shaft—check the instructions), door hinges (especially those on swinging doors), window sash locks and cranks (if you have them), toilet-seat hinges, the kitchen exhaust fan, small motors on appliances (check instructions), the oil burner motor and circulation pump or blower (*warning:* don't overlube these), and tools (a light coat over their metal surfaces prevents rust).
- Heavier machine oil (number 20) in a squirt can
  — Use on attic fan (see instructions), on rollers and pulleys of overhead garage doors.
- Commercial stick lube (candle stub, paraffin, or soap also will do)
  — Use on door latches, window casement and jalousie channels (work the window to spread it), drawer slides, friction catches on kitchen cabinets.
- Powdered graphite
  — Blow into door locks, use on window shade mechanisms, on the tracks of overhead garage doors.
- Aerosol spray lubricant (containing fluorocarbon) with spray straw

— Use on channels of double-hung windows as well as channels of combo storm and screen windows; tracks of sliding closet, furniture, shower, and medicine cabinet doors; sliding parts of drapery traverse rods and moving parts of venetian blinds. Also works in door locks.

REPAIRING A LEAKING FAUCET

A small faucet drip can leak up to five thousand gallons of water per year. If it's hot water, add the cost of energy to heat that much water. Dripping faucets also stain sinks, and if you're trying to go to sleep nearby, forget it.

What You Need

- A box of assorted-size washers (unless you know the size)
- A screwdriver
- An adjustable wrench

How to Do It

1. First turn off the water at the shutoff valve nearest the faucet you are going to repair. Then turn on the faucet until the water stops flowing (see fig. 7-3).

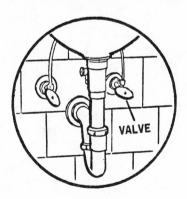

Fig. 7–3

2. Loosen the packing nut with a wrench. Most nuts loosen by turning counterclockwise (see fig. 7-4). Use the faucet handle to pull out the valve unit (see fig. 7-5).

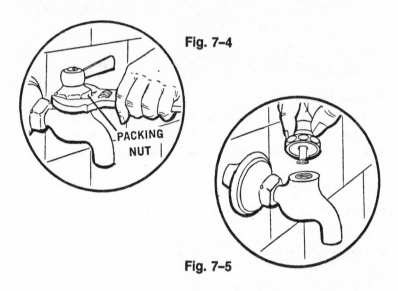

Fig. 7–4

Fig. 7–5

3. Remove the screw holding the old washer at the bottom of the valve unit (see fig. 7-6).

Fig. 7–6

4. Put in the new washer and replace the screw (see fig. 7-7).

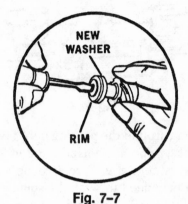

Fig. 7-7

5. Put the valve unit back in the faucet. Turn the handle to the proper position.

6. Tighten the packing nut (see fig. 7-8).

Fig. 7-8

7. Turn on the water at the shutoff valve.

Faucets may look different, but they are all built about the same. Mixing faucets (see fig. 7-9), which are used on sinks, laundry tubs, and bathtubs are two separate units with the same spout. You'll need to repair each unit separately.

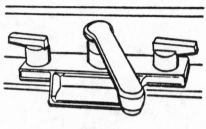

Fig. 7–9

Is water leaking around the packing nut? Try tightening the nut. If it still leaks, remove the handle and loosen the packing nut. If there is a washer under it, replace the washer. If there's no washer, you may need to wrap the spindle with "packing wicking" (see fig. 7-10). Then replace the packing nut and handle and turn the water back on at the shutoff valve.

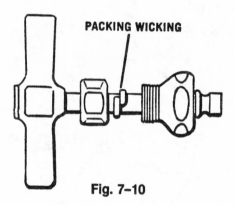

PACKING WICKING

Fig. 7–10

FILLING THE CRACKS AROUND BATHTUB OR SHOWER

A crack between the bathtub and wall may look harmless enough, but leaking water can damage the walls and house frame. Whenever you notice such a crack, don't let anyone bathe or shower until you fix it.

What You Need
There are two types of waterproof crack filler. Choose one.

- Waterproof grout, which comes in powder form. It must be mixed with water. You can mix it in small amounts at a time. Grout costs less than plastic sealers.
- Plastic sealer, which comes in a tube. It looks like toothpaste and is easier to use than grout but costs more. Read the directions on the package before you begin your project.

How to Do It

Prepare the surface

1. Remove the old crack filler from the crack (see fig. 7-11).

Fig. 7–11

2. Wash the surface to remove soap, grease, and dirt (see fig. 7-12).

Fig. 7–12

3. Dry the surface well before you make repairs (see fig. 7-13).

Fig. 7-13

Using grout

1. Put a small amount of grout in a bowl. Slowly add water and mix until you have a thick paste (see fig. 7-14). Put this mixture in the crack with a putty knife (see fig. 7-15). Press in to fill the crack (see fig. 7-16). Smooth the surface (see fig. 7-17).

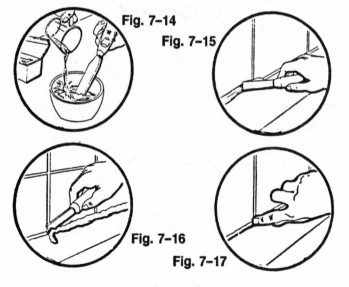

Fig. 7-14

Fig. 7-15

Fig. 7-16

Fig. 7-17

2. Wipe excess grout from the wall and tub before it gets dry and hard. Let the grout dry well before anyone uses the tub.

3. Empty any leftover grout mixture (but *not* down the drain). Wash the bowl and knife before grout dries on them.

Using plastic sealer

1. Squeeze plastic sealer from the tube in a ribbon along the crack (see fig. 7-18).

Fig. 7–18

2. Use a putty knife or spatula to press it down and fill the crack. Smooth the surface. Work fast! This stuff dries in a very few minutes.

3. Keep the cap on the tube when you're not using it.

SETTING TILE—FLEXIBLE, CERAMIC, OR PLASTIC?

Tiles that come loose from walls or floors can cause adjoining tiles to follow suit. They can also make any surface look shoddy. And if they're ceramic tiles on a tub or shower, water leaking in can severely damage the structure of the house. This is the kind of small repair job that it's hard to hire someone to do.

What You Need

- A mixing bowl
- Tile adhesive for the kind of tile you have
- Paint brush or putty knife
- Knife or saw
- New tile (if needed)
- Grout—for ceramic or plastic tile
- Rolling pin (optional)

How to Do It

Flexible tile

1. Remove loose or damaged tile. A warm iron will help soften the adhesive (see fig. 7-19).

Fig. 7–19

2. Scrape off the old adhesive from the floor or wall (see fig. 7-20). Also from the tile if you're using it again.

Fig. 7–20

3. Fit tiles carefully. Some tile can be cut with a knife or shears, others with a saw (see fig. 7-21). Tile is less apt to break if it is warm.

Fig. 7–21

4. Spread adhesive on the floor or wall with a paint brush or putty knife (see fig. 7-22).

Fig. 7–22

5. Wait until the adhesive begins to set before placing the tile.
6. Press the tile on firmly. A rolling pin works well (see fig. 7-23).

Fig. 7–23

Ceramic or plastic tile

1. Scrape the old adhesive off the floor or wall (see fig. 7-24). Also from the old tile if you are reusing it.

Fig. 7–24

2. If you are using new tile and need to fit it, mark it carefully to size. Cut it with a saw. You can make straight cuts on ceramic tile by scoring it first. Then it will snap off if you press it on the edge of a hard surface (see fig. 7-25).

Fig. 7–25

3. Spread adhesive on the wall or floor and on the back of the tile. Press the tile firmly into place (see fig. 7-26).

Fig. 7–26

4. Joints on ceramic tile should be filled with grout after the tile has firmly set. Mix grout (powder) with water to form a stiff paste. Press the mixture into the joints with your fingers (see fig. 7-27). Smooth the surface.

Fig. 7–27

5. Carefully remove excess grout from the tile surface before it dries (see fig. 7-28).

Fig. 7–28

6. Clean up surfaces, bowl, and tools before the grout dries (see fig. 7-29).

Fig. 7–29

7. Let the grout dry overnight before it gets wet again.

PATCHING HOLES IN WALLBOARD OR PLASTER

Holes and cracks in walls can only get worse. In outside walls they can also let in winter chill or summer heat. Repairing them immediately stops further damage and keeps appearances as they should be.

What You Need

- One of the two types of patching compounds, both of which need to be mixed with water:
  — Spackling compound is convenient for small jobs but is more expensive. It can be bought as a powder or ready-mixed in a can.
  — Patching plaster can be bought in larger packages and costs less.
- Putty knife
- Knife
- Sandpaper—medium grit
- Old cloth or a paintbrush

How to Do It

1. Remove any loose plaster. With a knife, scrape out plaster from the back edges of the crack until the back of the crack is wider than the front surface (see fig. 7-30).

Fig. 7–30

2. Thoroughly dampen the surface of the crack with a wet cloth or paintbrush (see fig. 7-31).

Fig. 7–31

3. Prepare the patching compound according to the directions on the package (see fig. 7-32). Mix only a small amount the first time.

Fig. 7–32

4. You can fill small holes with the patching mixture. Be sure to press the mixture until it completely fills the hole. Smooth the surface with a putty knife (see fig. 7-33). After the patch has dried, you can sand it. Wrap the sandpaper around a small piece of wood (see fig. 7-34). This makes the surface even.

Fig. 7–33

Fig. 7–34

5. Larger holes or cracks should be filled step by step. First, partly fill the hole. Let the patch dry. This gives a base for the final fill. Add a second batch of compound (see fig. 7-35). Let dry. Sand until smooth.

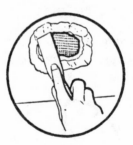

Fig. 7–35

6. You may need to fill in behind large holes with wadded newspaper. Start patching by working in from all sides. Let dry. Apply another layer around the new edge. Repeat until the hole is filled (see fig. 7-36). After the patch has dried, sand until smooth.

Fig. 7–36

Note: If the walls have a textured surface, you'll want to make the patch match them while the plaster is still wet. You might need a sponge or comb to do the texturing (see fig. 7-37).

Fig. 7–37

ELECTRIC PLUGS—REPAIR OR REPLACE?

Lamps that flicker or appliances that won't work until you wiggle the plug are safety hazards—they can set your house on fire or electrocute you. Sure, you can disconnect them and take them to an electrician and usually pay a reasonable fee, or you can take care of it yourself . . . in about the time it'd take you to drive to the repair shop.

What You Need

- New plug—if your old one cannot be used (buy one with an Underwriters Laboratories/UL label)

- Screwdriver
- Knife

How to Do It

1. Cut the cord off at the damaged part (see fig. 7-38).

Fig. 7–38

2. Slip the plug back on the cord (see fig. 7-39).

Fig. 7–39

3. Clip and separate the cord (see fig. 7-40).

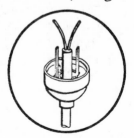

Fig. 7–40

4. Tie Underwriters' knot (see fig. 7-41).

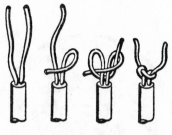

Fig. 7-41

5. Remove a half inch of the insulation from the end of the wires, being sure not to cut any of the small strands of wires (see fig. 7-42).

Fig. 7-42

6. Twist the small wires together, clockwise (see fig. 7-43).

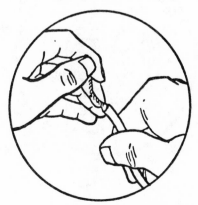

Fig. 7-43

7. Pull the knot down firmly in the plug (see fig. 7-44).

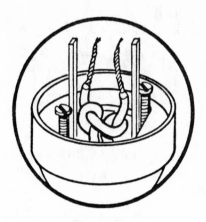

Fig. 7–44

8. Pull one wire around each terminal to the screw (see fig. 7-45).

Fig. 7–45

9. Wrap the wire around the screw, clockwise (see fig. 7-46).

Fig. 7–46

10. Tighten the screw. Insulation should come to the screw but not under it (see fig. 7-47).

Fig. 7–47

11. Place the insulation cover back over the plug (see fig. 7-48).

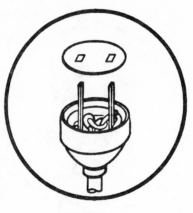

Fig. 7–48

Repairing Drawers

There is no reason to let a drawer that sticks or a drawer without a handle put a piece of furniture out of commission.

What You Need

• Screwdriver
• Sandpaper
• Candle wax or paraffin (soap also will do)

How to Do It

For loose handles and knobs

1. Tighten handles or knobs with a screwdriver from the inside of the drawer (see fig. 7-49).

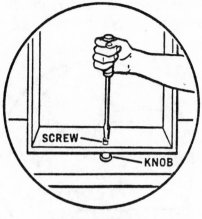

Fig. 7–49

2. You can buy knobs or use small spools to replace lost knobs.

For sticking drawers

1. Remove the drawer. Look for shiny places on top or bottom edges or on the sides where the drawer is sticking (see fig. 7-50).

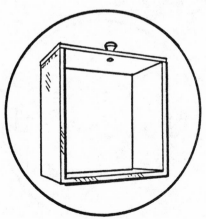

Fig. 7–50

2. Sand down these shiny areas. Try the drawer to see if it moves more easily. Repeat the sanding if it still sticks (see fig. 7-51).

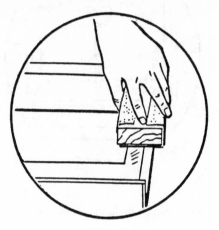

Fig. 7–51

3. Rub the drawer and the frame where they rub with candle wax, paraffin, or soap. This makes drawers glide easier, which is especially important if drawers are filled with heavy items (see fig. 7-52).

CANDLE WAX

Fig. 7–52

4. If the glides are badly worn, the drawer may not close all the way. The drawer front strikes the frame. The drawer needs to be lifted. Remove it and insert two or three large smooth-head thumbtacks along the front of each glide (see fig. 7-53).

Fig. 7–53

5. Do the drawers stick only in damp weather? When the weather is dry and the drawers are not sticking, coat the unfinished wood with a penetrating sealer or with wax (see fig. 7-54).

Fig. 7–54

FIXING PROBLEM DOORS

Doors that won't close or catch and those that squeak or stick are more of a nuisance than anything; doors to unheated rooms that won't close increase your heating bill. They should be fixed to keep your house running efficiently.

What You Need

- Light oil
- Graphite
- Wood glue
- Screwdriver
- Hammer
- Sandpaper
- Pliers

How to Do It

- Usually you can stop a door squeak by putting a few drops of oil at the top of each hinge. Move the door back and forth to work the oil into the hinge. If the squeaking does not stop, raise the pin and add more oil (see fig. 7-55).

Fig. 7–55

- Noisy or squeaking locks should be lubricated with graphite (see fig. 7-56). You can buy this at a hardware store. A lock that's tight or won't turn also needs graphite.

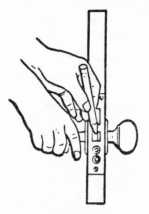

Fig. 7–56

- To stop a rattle in the knob, loosen the set screw on the knob (see fig. 7-57). Remove the knob. Put a small piece of putty or modeling clay in the knob (see fig. 7-58). Replace the knob. Push it on as far as possible. Tighten the screw.

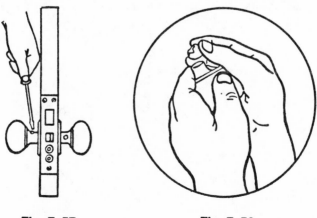

Fig. 7–57　　　　　　　**Fig. 7–58**

For sticking or dragging doors

1. Tighten screws in the hinges. If screws are not holding, replace them, one at a time, with longer screws. Or insert a glue-covered matchstick in the hole and put the old screw back in (see fig. 7-59).

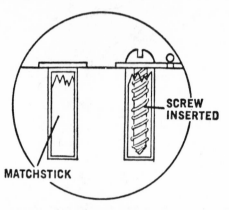

Fig. 7–59

2. Look for a shiny spot on the door where it sticks. Open and close the door slowly to find the spot. Sand down the shiny spot (see fig. 7-60). Do not sand too much or the door will not fit as tightly as it should.

Fig. 7–60

3. If the door or frame is badly out of shape, you may have to remove the door and plane down the part that drags (see fig. 7-61).

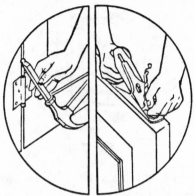

Fig. 7-61

4. Sand the edges of the door before painting to prevent a paint buildup. This can cause a door to stick.

REPLACING A BROKEN WINDOW/SEALING AROUND WINDOW GLASS

Besides being unsightly, a broken window can make breaking into your home easier, cause heat loss, and admit rain, dust, and insects. Also, putty that is missing or dried out can lessen the insulation value of your windows.

What You Need

- Window glass (correct size)
- Putty or glazing compound
- Putty knife
- Hammer
- Pliers
- Glazier points

How to Replace a Broken Window

1. Work from the outside of the frame (see fig. 7-62).

Fig. 7–62

2. Remove the broken glass with pliers to avoid cutting your fingers (see fig. 7-63).

Fig. 7–63

3. Remove old putty and glazier points. Pliers also will help do this (see fig. 7-64).

Fig. 7–64

4. Place a thin ribbon of putty in the frame (see fig. 7-65).

Fig. 7–65

5. Place the glass firmly against the putty (see fig. 7-66).

Fig. 7–66

6. Insert the glazier points. Place the head of a screwdriver against the glazier point and tap the screwdriver handle carefully to prevent breaking the glass. The points should be placed near the corners first and then every four to six inches along the glass (see fig. 7-67).

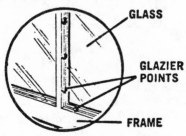

Fig. 7–67

7. Fill the groove with putty or glazing compound. Press it firmly against the glass with a putty knife or with your fingers. Smooth the surface with the putty knife. The putty should form a smooth seal around the window (see fig. 7-68).

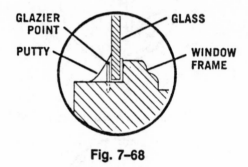

GLAZIER POINT   GLASS

PUTTY   WINDOW FRAME

Fig. 7–68

How to Reseal Glass

1. To seal around glass in windows and doors, use putty and apply with a putty knife (see fig. 7-69).

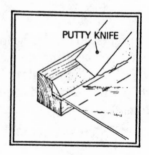

PUTTY KNIFE

Fig. 7–69

2. Lay a small roll of putty, one-eighth inch to one-quarter inch thick, around the sash or frame so that it fills the groove in which the glass rests. Make sure that the putty is fully applied to both the glass and the sash or frame.

3. Press the putty firmly with the knife to assure a good seal. Trim away excess as you work.

REPAIRING SCREENS

There's no need to have a whole screen replaced just because there's a hole in it, but there is a need to mend the hole. Small holes tend to become larger, and insects can enter the house.

What You Need

- Screening or ready-cut screen patches
- Shears
- A ruler or small block of wood with a straight edge
- Fine wire or nylon thread

How to Do It

1. Trim the hole in the screen to make smooth edges (see fig. 7-70).

Fig. 7-70

2. Cut a rectangular patch of screen an inch larger than the hole.
3. Remove the three outside wires on all four sides of the patch (see fig. 7-71).

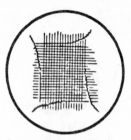

Fig. 7–71

4. Bend the ends of the wires out. An easy way is to bend them over a block of wood or the edge of a ruler (see fig. 7-72).

Fig. 7–72

5. Put the patch over the hole from the outside. Hold it tight against the screen so that the small, bent wire ends go through the screen (see fig. 7-73).

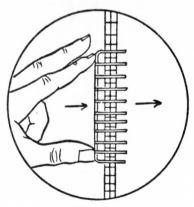

Fig. 7–73

6. From inside, bend down the ends of the wires toward the center of the hole. You may need someone outside to press against the patch while you do this (see fig. 7-74).

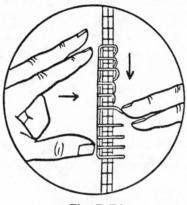

Fig. 7–74

7. You can mend *small* holes by stitching back and forth with a fine wire or a nylon thread (see fig. 7-75). Use a matching color.

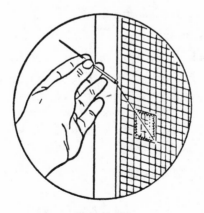

Fig. 7–75

CAULKING AND FILLING CRACKS IN EXTERIOR OF HOUSE

Cracks in the exterior of your house are directly related to increased heating and cooling bills; increased moisture, dust, and dirt entering the house; and increased insect activity in the house. Don't dismiss tiny escape outlets as inconsequential. Combined, they could be the equivalent of a one-square-foot hole.

What You Need

- Putty (synthetic)—can be oil-based (which lasts a year), acrylic latex (ten years), or silicone (twenty years)
- Putty knife
- Caulking compound (polyvinyl acetate type, in both rope and bulk form). Caulk is an elastic, adhesive material that is squeezed from a tube into gaps and seams where different types and sizes of building materials meet, or where pipes and wires enter your house.
- Packaged, ready-mixed mortar (if repairing masonry walls)
- Solvent, such as cleaning fluid
- Small pointing trowel
- Chisel (small, narrow blade, with steel-capped handle)
- Masonry joint finishing tool (if repairing masonry walls and the existing masonry joints are "concave" joints)

How to Caulk Cracks and Holes (Nonmasonry)

- Check the following places for cracks and holes that need caulking:
  — Between window and door frames and the main frame of the house (see fig. 7-76)

Fig. 7–76

— Gaps in sidings and at corners of the house (see fig. 7-77)

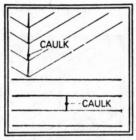

Fig. 7–77

— Joints formed by siding and masonry (see fig. 7-78)

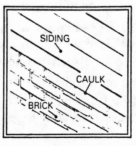

Fig. 7–78

— The underside of eaves where wall and eave meet (see fig. 7-79)

Fig. 7–79

— The joints where steps and porches meet the house (see fig. 7-80)

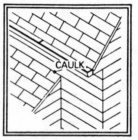

Fig. 7–80

— The surface of wood siding, trim, fascias
- Before applying new caulking (or putty), remove the old and wipe the area clean with a cloth soaked with a solvent similar to cleaning fluid such as Energine.
- Caulk comes in three forms:
  — Rope form (see fig. 7-81); unwind the caulk and force it into the cracks with your fingers.

Fig. 7–81

— Bulk; this is applied with a putty knife or small trowel (see fig. 7-82); good for large openings or cracks, such as gaps between lengths of siding.

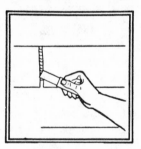

Fig. 7–82

— Disposable cartridges, the most popular, which have a plastic tip or nozzle that is tapered so you can control the size of the bead (by how far back from the tip you cut the end off); these cartridges fit into a half-barrel caulking gun that has a trigger-activated plunger that forces the caulk out.

How to Fill Masonry Cracks

1. Using the chisel, chip out loose mortar from all joints to be filled.
2. Mix a batch of mortar according to the directions on the package.

3. Wet the masonry thoroughly before you begin and keep it wet as you work.

4. Apply the mortar with a small pointing trowel (see fig. 7-83). Press the mortar firmly into the joint, making sure the joint is full.

Fig. 7–83

5. Take off the excess mortar with the edge of the trowel. Now finish the joint to match the existing joints (see fig. 7-84). You can make the V shape with the tip of the pointing trowel. Hold the trowel at a forty-five-degree angle to the joint, push the tip into the joint, and then firmly move the trowel along the joint (see fig. 7-85).

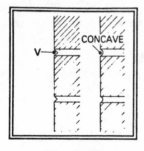

Fig. 7–84

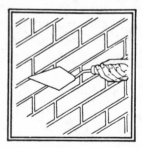

Fig. 7–85

You'll need a special masonry tool called a "jointer" to make a concave joint (see fig. 7-86). The concave joint is formed by placing the jointer over the mortar joint length-wise and pressing the mortar firmly into the joint to form the concave shape (see fig. 7-87).

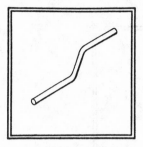

Fig. 7–86

Fig. 7–87

6. Fill and finish a joint (equal to eight to ten brick lengths) before you start another.

7. Keep the newly filled joints damp for two or three days by frequently wetting with a fine spray from a water hose or by covering with wet burlap.

FIXING CRACKS IN CONCRETE SIDEWALKS OR DRIVEWAYS

Small cracks in sidewalks, if not patched, become larger and can eventually lead to dangerous, uneven surfaces. In the early stages, they're simple to repair.

What You Need

- Packaged, ready-mixed mortar
- Epoxy concrete ("clear" type for narrow cracks and "gray" type for wide cracks and concrete breaks)
- Wire brush
- Pointing trowel and wood float
- Heavy-duty paintbrush

How to Do It

1. *Caution!* Repair only when concrete is dry.
2. Chisel out the crack or hole at an angle, making it wider under the surface (see fig. 7-88).

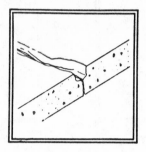

Fig. 7–88

3. Clean the concrete surface thoroughly with the wire brush (see fig. 7-89).

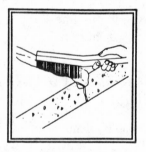

Fig. 7–89

4. Mix a batch of mortar according to the directions on the package. Mix the epoxy concrete with the mortar according to the directions on the epoxy container.
5. Using the trowel, put the mixture into the crack (see fig. 7-90).

Fig. 7-90

6. Using the wood float, smooth the mixture even with the concrete surface (see fig. 7-91).

Fig. 7-91

7. Clean the tools immediately with paint thinner.

- Work fast! Most epoxies will harden in an hour. If the patch should harden before the operation is completed, apply a second coat and smooth the surface again.

- For big cracks, spread the mixture over the full width of the crack until the level of mortar is slightly above the concrete surface.

- If repairing a full break in the concrete, use the trowel to force the mortar mixture to the bottom of the break (see fig. 7-92).

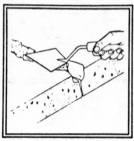

Fig. 7–92

MAINTAINING METAL GUTTERS AND DOWNSPOUTS

If water stands in the gutter, over time it can rust a hole in it. If water overflows or spills over the edge or leaks from the gutter or downspout, it can do serious damage to the house. The purpose of gutters is to carry water away from the house and avoid wood rot and paint failure. It's important to keep gutters doing their job.

What You Need

- Ladder
- Metal gutter straps (straps must be the same type of metal as your existing gutters and straps)
- Galvanized or aluminum spikes (if required instead of straps)
- Galvanized or aluminum screws and nails
- Asphalt roofing cement
- Hammer and screwdriver
- Plumber's snake (or flexible metal cable, approximately one-quarter inch in diameter)

- Wire brush
- Putty knife (or flat piece of scrap wood)
- Canvas patch

How to Clean Them and Adjust Tightness

1. Inspect and clean gutters and downspouts at least twice annually.
2. Remove all leaves and other debris from the gutters and check for loose joints (see fig. 7-93).

Fig. 7–93

3. Check the gutter outlet opening where the water flows into the downspout. The outlet should have either a leaf guard or leaf strainer. Clean debris from the leaf guard or strainer and replace in position (see fig. 7-94).

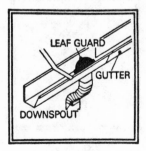

Fig. 7–94

4. Check all gutter hangings for tightness. If the hanger is a "strap" type and is loose, renail it with a galvanized nail or tighten it with a galvanized screw. Broken or damaged straps should be replaced (see fig. 7-95). If the hanger is a "sleeve and spike" type and is loose, renail it with a galvanized or aluminum spike (see fig. 7-96).

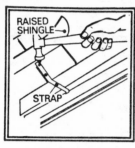 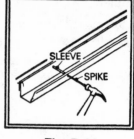

Fig. 7–95   **Fig. 7–96**

5. Pour water into each gutter, using a hose or a pail of water. As the water flows, check each gutter for proper water-drainage and for leaks.

6. Check each downspout for water flow and for leaks.

7. Should water stoppage occur in the downspout, clean the downspout at the gutter outlet using a plumber's snake or a piece of flexible metal cable (see fig. 7-97).

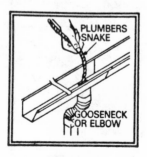

Fig. 7–97

How to Adjust the Pitch

Should the water not drain completely from the gutter, the gutter hangers should be adjusted to give proper slope to the gutter.

Strap-type hanger

1. If the hanger is a strap type, lift the edge of the shingle or other roofing material to expose the strap end.

2. Remove the end of the strap from the roof (see fig. 7-98).

3. Then unscrew or unsnap the attached end of the strap from the gutter (see fig. 7-99).

Fig. 7–98   **Fig. 7–99**

4. Raise the strap to a higher position on the roof and renail it to the roof with galvanized nails (see fig. 7-100). Make certain that the new nail is located at least three-quarters inch from the old nail hole to avoid weakening the new nail hole.

Fig. 7–100

5. Cover the nailheads with a dab of asphalt cement.
6. Now raise the gutter into position and fasten the remaining end of the strap to the gutter.

Sleeve and spike type hanger

1. A different procedure is required if the hanger is a sleeve and spike type. You must free the gutter by cutting the spike with a hacksaw blade (see fig. 7-101).

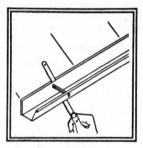

Fig. 7–101

2. Place the sleeve in another, adjacent location, at least three-quarters inch from the old location.

3. Raise the gutter and refasten it to the roof board by nailing a new galvanized spike through the sleeve and into the board (back to fig. 7-96).

How to Repair Small Leaks

1. Once you locate the leak, use the wire brush to clean the area of the leak free of loose metal and rust (see fig. 7-102). Then wipe clean with a cloth.

Fig. 7–102

2. Using a putty knife, apply asphalt roofing cement over the leak area and spread it with the knife (see fig. 7-103).

Fig. 7–103

3. Clean the putty knife with solvent or a similar cleaning fluid.

How to Repair Larger Cracks
If the crack or hole is greater than one-quarter inch, use the technique described in the following two steps:

1. Cut a small piece of canvas one-half to three-quarters inch larger than the hole.

2. Apply a thin layer of roofing cement over the leak area. Place the canvas patch over the cement and press it firmly. Now apply a second heavy coat of cement, fully covering the patch (see fig. 7-104).

Fig. 7–104

CHOOSING A PROFESSIONAL

Even if you try to do everything yourself, chances are you'll have to hire a professional from time to time. Just as you have to go about a do-it-yourself job correctly, there are correct procedures for commissioning work. What is essential is that you find a good repairman, set exact specifications for what needs to be done, and get it in writing.

Job Specifications

Before you contact a professional, figure out the kind and quality of the repair needed. This ensures that you get what you want, clarifies communication with whomever you hire, and protects you from switcheroo tactics in which a lower price is offered in the beginning to sell you and then you're persuaded into switching to a more costly product.

To reach a clear and binding agreement you should know and write down in detail what you expect for the amount of money you are to pay; then you and the repairman can make adjustments. Don't overspend, but plan to use quality materials, since labor often will be your main cost. Make sure the following are specified:

- The exact location and extent of the repair
- Indication of any repairs that are to be made beforehand if the job involves new work (for example, putting new siding on the house)

- Type and quality of materials to be used
- Color and sizes of materials
- If painting, exactly what areas or surfaces are to be painted and number of coats to be applied
- Agreement that the work shall conform to local and state codes

The Contract

An agreement between you and the contractor must be executed. In addition to the specifications above, it should describe:

- All material, labor, and equipment necessary for the job. (If painting, then the types, brands, and quality of paints to be used and the number of coats, including primer coats, to be applied. Professional painters usually offer three grades of paint jobs: premium, standard, and minimum.)
- When the job is to be completed, allowing for possible delays (because of bad weather, for example).
- Who cleans up the mess that results from the job.
- The amount to which a repairman or contractor shall assume responsibility for damage to your property or that of your neighbors. (If painting, the measures to be taken to protect the floors, furnishings, and other parts of the house.)
- That any changes in the contract shall be made in writing and agreed to by both parties.
- That the agreement frees you from all liens that may be placed against the job for failure of the contractor/repairman to pay for materials, labor, or equipment.
- That he is adequately insured as required by pertinent local regulations; otherwise, you could be held liable for accidents that might occur on your property.
- The specific price for the job and a schedule of how and when payments are to be made.

A Few More Suggestions

- Try to select a repairman or contractor whose work you or your neighbors and friends know. Examine some of his previous work and ask the owners if they are satisfied. If you need help, consult an architect, businessman, or the Better Business Bureau in your area. Seek at least three bids before you choose a contractor.

- You may wish to check on the work in progress. However, stay out of the way. Interference can cause delays, affect the quality of the work, or cause disagreements and added costs.

- Afterward, inspect the project with whomever you hired. Test all fixtures, switches, windows, doors, etc. If there are questions, refer to the contract. About the only leverage you have at this point is withholding your final payment. Sign the contract and make final payment only after all the work has been completed correctly.

- About your only recourse if you and a contractor come to an impasse is to file a report with the Better Business Bureau and see a lawyer. If the job was small and within the jurisdiction of small claims court (it varies from state to state—New York, for example, has a limit of fifteen hundred dollars), you have that option.

Chapter 8

AROUND THE HOUSE: HOW EVERYTHING WORKS AND HOW YOU CAN MAKE IT WORK MORE EFFICIENTLY

A house is comprised of various systems. Viewing them as a complex whole can be intimidating—all that mishmash of wires and pipes going every which way connecting boilers, pumps, hot-water heaters, and other things you can't even identify. Not understanding what makes your house tick puts you at the mercy of repairmen and contractors—some scrupulous, some not.

Not understanding also keeps you from maintaining your equipment. Homeowners must practice preventive maintenance, best summed up by the adage "A stitch in time saves nine." No piece of household equipment suddenly gives out. There always are indicators—strange noises, wheezes, grindings—that signal trouble. Preventive maintenance keeps you apprised, lengthens equipment life, and saves you lots of money. Chapter 6, *"The VHH* Timetable," organizes and schedules the activities necessary to maintain the house totally year round. Here we get down to the details of how to maintain it.

THE ELECTRICAL SYSTEM

How It Works

Two or three heavy wires lead into your home. Two wires give the house a 120-volt system; three make 240 volts available. Most heavy appliances operate on 240 volts. Volts are not electric current (amperes are); like water pressure, volts force current through the line, so the more voltage you have, the greater the current flow. Simply put, electricity is a combination of amperage, the current flow, and voltage, the pressure to force the amps through the wire. You'll also run across the term wattage: Watts are equal to volts multiplied by amps and represent the amount of power required by an appliance or a device, such as a 100-watt lightbulb. A 120-volt system protected by a 15-amp fuse or circuit breaker can supply 1,800 (120 × 15) watts.

Homeowners can be baffled by irregular wall outlets that were installed for a specific appliance (often an air conditioner or other heavy-duty appliance). If you have one or several of these, fig. 8-1 will enable you to determine the voltage and amp fuse by the outlet.

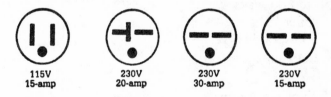

| 115V | 230V | 230V | 230V |
| 15-amp | 20-amp | 30-amp | 15-amp |

Fig. 8–1

Household Appliances and Wattages They Consume

To give you an idea of the draw on your wiring, here are some common household appliances and approximately how much they draw. Standard household wiring usually can handle no more than 1,500 watts on a regular circuit.

- 15 to 100 watts:
  — bottle warmer
  — can opener
  — clock
  — electric fan
  — heating pad

— knife sharpener
— light bulbs
— radio
— record player
— sewing machine
— shaver
— table lamps
— vacuum cleaner

- 150 to 300 watts:
— blender
— electric blanket
— hair dryer
— mixer
— refrigerator
— three-way lamps
— window fan

- 350 to 800 watts:
— coffee maker
— floor polisher
— sun lamp
— TV

- 1,000 or more watts:
— broiler
— corn popper
— deep fat fryer
— electric iron
— electric skillet
— portable oven
— space heater
— toaster
— waffle iron

Service Entry

The wires running to the house are called service entrance wires and pass directly into a meter that the utility company uses to measure the amount of electricity you consume. From the meter the wires lead inside to a service panel where fuses or circuit breakers are located. (Most modern systems are controlled by circuit breakers.) There is also a main switch or a fuse bank that can be pulled to cut all the power. Every member of the household should know where this is located in case of an emergency such as an electrical fire, or a person being electrocuted.

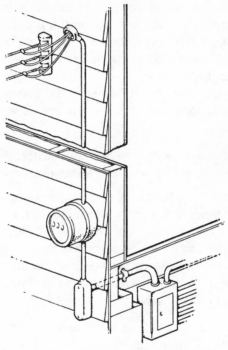

Fig. 8-2

Circuit Breakers and Fuses

See fig. 8-2 above—from the service center (fuse box or circuit breaker board) the wires go their separate ways throughout the house to various outlets and fixtures where electricity will be used. Wires leaving the service center are divided into groups called circuits, and each group is controlled by a fuse or by a circuit breaker. This branch-out of wires spreads the electrical load so no single circuit is overloaded; it enables you to shut off current to various sections of the house; it monitors overload or misuse by blowing fuses and tripping circuits; and it provides extra power on special lines to heavy-duty appliances such as stoves and electric dryers.

There are limits on how much electricity wires can carry. A thick wire can carry a heavier current than a thin one. If too much current is forced through a wire, the wire can overheat, burn through its insulation, and start a fire. Besides an overloaded circuit, if two exposed wires touch, either in the wiring or in an appliance, a short circuit can result, and this can catch a house on fire as well.

Enter fuses and circuit breakers: To protect wiring from overheating, they shut off the current. The mechanism is simple:

- A circuit breaker looks like a wall switch. An overload or a short trips the switch, which moves from on to off.

- A fuse contains a strip of metal with a prescribed melting point that becomes part of the circuit. (You can see the strip through the window on the fuse.) A short or overload causes the strip to melt and breaks the circuit. (A fuse that has blown because of an overload usually shows a clear window and a broken wire; a short-circuited fuse usually has a blackened or discolored window.)

Besides the regular plug fuses there are two other kinds of fuses worth mentioning:

- Time-delay fuses allow for a heavy draw of power while an appliance or motor is starting up.

- Screw-in breakers have a button that pops out when the fuse is blown and can be pushed in to reset.

To get back in business, first turn off or unplug whatever it was you think might have blown the fuse or circuit breaker. It makes no sense to reset a circuit breaker or replace a blown fuse unless you find and correct the cause of trouble. In most cases it is too many appliances on the same circuit.

It's best to turn off the house main switch before changing a fuse. Remove the fuse by turning it counterclockwise, then replace with a fuse of the same capacity. The rim of the fuse is insulated and is the only part of the fuse (or fuse box) you should touch when you replace a burn-out.

One danger with ordinary fuses is that they can be replaced with fuses of heavier capacity. Doing this can be equated with bolting down a steam boiler's safety valve. It defeats the purpose of a fuse, which is supposed to blow before an overload starts a wiring fire. Ideally the washer, drier, fridge, dishwasher, water pump, and other major appliances that are heavy power-drawers should have circuits to themselves, usually 20 amps or more.

A chart or labels should identify each circuit at the fuse-box/circuit-breaker box site. This is a quick job, especially with two people. One roams the house turning on lights and appliances, plugging a light into outlets, and yelling what goes off when. The other person unscrews fuses or flicks circuit breakers and writes it all down. Why do you need a chart? It saves time if you or an electrician need to do any work on a circuit. And if you ever need to turn it off in a hurry, you'll be able to. (In a real emergency, however, use the main switch.)

YOUR PLUMBING SYSTEM

The home plumbing system is comprised of two parts:

- a freshwater system consisting of hot- and cold-water pipes that supply the house
- a vented drainage, waste, or sewer system that carries waste from the house to street sewer, septic tank, or cesspool

Components of the Freshwater System

- Water-supply pipes are relatively small, with inside diameters from three-eighths to one inch. The incoming pipe splits at the hot-water heater into hot- and cold-water systems. Pipes for the two usually run parallel throughout the house. Water is carried under pressure created by either a well pump in a private system or by gravity in the public municipal water supply system (to obtain pressure they usually store the water in standpipes (a.k.a. water towers) that often have the name of your municipality written on them.

- Shutoff valves—these control the flow of water to various parts of the system. Water can be shut off at three stages along the way. First there's a main shutoff valve that cuts off the *entire* water supply. Then there are branch shutoff valves that control the flow to various areas and fixtures. Generally you can shut off the hot-water supply for the whole house at the hot-water heater. Finally, leading into each fixture or faucet is yet another valve.

Note: Main and branch shutoff valves should be labeled. Then in case of any emergency, time won't be lost frantically looking for the proper valve to turn off.

Components of the DWV (drain/waste/vent) system:

- These pipes are larger than incoming water-supply pipes, with diameters varying from 1¼ to four inches, and they rely on gravity to bring waste water away from the fixtures. The entire system is pitched slightly downward so that waste flowing out of a fixture will flow through the pipes and out of the house.

- At each fixture are curved U- or S-shaped sections of pipe called traps. A trap retains water that in turn acts as a seal to prevent sewer gases, bacteria, and vermin from entering the house. Traps are also the point in the drainage system most likely to get clogged. They are readily accessible under sinks and lavatories; traps for showers and bathtubs can sometimes be reached from the floor below if they are over a crawl space or unfinished basement; toilets have built-in traps.

- While the drain system goes downward, a vent pipe system goes up (notice roof vent pipes in every house you see). Vent pipes not only carry off sewer gases but also keep the whole DWV system at atmospheric pressure, which is necessary to maintain that water seal in each trap.

Maintenance
There is not a lot to maintaining a plumbing system.

- If you have your own water pump, keep it oiled as indicated in the owner's manual.

- A hot-water heater should be drained periodically (see page 78). And it can be made more energy-efficient with a good insulation jacket. If hot-water heaters are layered with enough insulation and padding, this can reduce heat loss by 80 percent and save 10 percent of the fuel the heater normally uses. You can go a step farther by getting a timer that turns it on and off in accordance with peak periods of hot-water usage.

- Showers and bathtubs should be equipped with screens that catch hair, bits of soap, etc., that can clog drain traps.

- Wipe as much grease as possible off pots and pans before washing them, and put a metal strainer in the drain to catch food particles. It's important that you keep as much solid matter and grease out of the drain as possible.

- Leaking faucets should be fixed at the first sign of a drip. The trouble usually is a worn washer (see pages 101–4 on how to fix this). If you keep wearing down the washer, you'll damage the valve seat (what the washer fits into to shut off the water).

- A garbage disposal doesn't necessarily grind up everything; often it just alters the form. If you have one, watch what you put down it. Pulpy foods such as asparagus and celery are transformed into fibrous masses that probably only Roto-Rooter or another expert will be able to remove.

Unclogging a Drain

Drain pipes increase in size as they run from fixtures to the main sewer pipe. It's important to remember this—an obstruction can often be pushed along until it reaches a larger pipe, then it can flow away and your troubles are over . . . until the next time.

Like house machinery, drains seldom stop up all at once. They get the "slows," which is your first indicator of trouble and is the best time to fix it. The blockage usually will be an accumulation of hair, grease, or other debris lodged somewhere near the drain. There are four ways to go after it:

- With a plunger (see page 61), a.k.a. a rubber force cup or a plumber's friend. Fill the basin with an inch or two of water (enough for the rim of the plunger to be underwater). Plug up the overflow opening with a wet cloth or have someone hold a hand tightly over it (this enables the plunger pressure to work on the obstruction instead of blowing out of the overflow outlet). A little petroleum jelly smeared on the cup edge assures a tighter seal. Place the suction cup over the drain and pump up and down on the plunger handle. The alternating pressure and suction created will often loosen the obstruction and push it to a larger-size pipe. When you feel it loosen, put plenty of water down the drain to send the obstruction on its way.

- With a liquid chemical drain cleaner. The solid cleaners, if not used properly, can solidify in the drain and make your problem even worse. *The VHH* recommends liquid and warns you to be sure to follow the instructions.

- With an adjustable wrench or pair of pliers, a piece of wire, and a bucket. Because the stoppage usually is in the trap, remove the small clean-out plug at the base (most traps have such a plug). Catch trap water in the bucket. Often you can work a piece of wire into the trap and pull out the obstruction. If the trap doesn't have a clean-out plug, remove the entire trap by loosening the two large nuts at each end.

Some newer traps are held by friction washers that will come off with a hard pull. If the drain remains clogged, with the trap removed, try either of the following.

- With a snake, a.k.a. a sink auger. This is a long coil of flexible steel with a point on the end. By rotating the snake into the drainpipe, it will generally cut its way through the obstruction and push it into the main sewer line, or enable you to pull it out.

- Also, a garden hose sometimes will do the job, with or without water pressure. Try it both ways.

The Flush Toilet

- How a flush tank works
  — That gizmo inside the toilet tank (see fig. 8-3) is not nearly as complicated as it looks. Here's what happens when you flush:

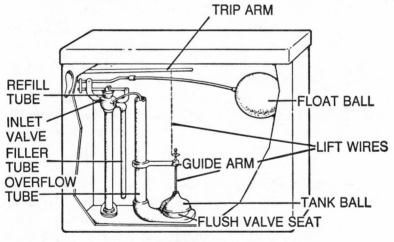

Fig. 8-3

1. The trip handle lifts the flush ball, allowing the water in the tank to empty into the toilet bowl.
2. The float ball falls with the tank water level, opening the inlet valve by a metal rod that is connected to the float. As

the inlet valve opens, the flush ball at the bottom drops back into place to shut off the flow of water into the tank.

3. The tank is filled through the filler tube. The toilet bowl is filled through the bowl refill tube, which flows into the overflow pipe to replenish trap-sealing water. (The overflow pipe feeds into the bowl, and if the tank gets too full of water, water will flow through the overflow into the bowl and then on out the drain.)

4. As the water reaches the top of the overflow pipe, the float shuts off the inlet valve and the cycle is complete.

- Troubleshooting
  — Water runs steadily into the tank. This problem is often stopped, but never prevented, by jiggling. Remove the tank top and watch the flushing mechanism in action. If the flush ball is not dropping squarely into the outlet seat (the hole where the water runs out), the trouble could be that the metal rods connecting the flush ball to the flush handle are not in alignment; they could be bent or not sliding through the guide attached to the overflow pipe. If the flush ball is falling back into place, check it and the valve seat for buildup of dirt, deposits, and rust that could be preventing a tight fit; they should be removed. The valve seat can be polished with steel wool or fine sandpaper. If the flush ball is hard or worn, replace it by unscrewing it from its rod.
  — Water runs steadily into the bowl. This indicates that the water supply to the tank isn't being shut off when it should be. Lift the float, and if that stops the water, try bending the float rod so the float will ride lower on the water and shut off the water sooner. If that doesn't stop it, the culprit might be an inlet valve washer that needs replacing. Tackle this if you feel up to it, or call a plumber. Often hardware stores or plumbing supply houses will sell you replacement parts and tell you how to install them.

— The tank won't flush, or the handle must be held down constantly when flushing. Is the flush handle loose? If so, tighten it. Is the bowl refill tube bent properly to allow water to go into the overflow pipe? If all this checks out, the flush ball may not be rising enough to let water flow freely out of the tank. Rebend the upper lift wire to lift the flush ball higher when the handle is activated.

- Unclogging one
  — Toilets have a built-in trap that curves back toward the front (see fig. 8-4). This is where trouble usually occurs. Chemical drain cleaners cannot penetrate the trap area, and therefore are ineffective.

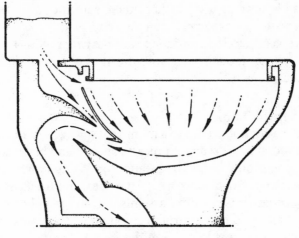

Fig. 8–4

1. Several minutes of plunging should do the trick. If they don't—

2. Try a coil-spring auger. This works on the same principle as a snake, but it has a crank handle attached to a housing with a sharp bend that gets the snake started in the toilet trap. Aim the auger into the trap area and turn the handle. Try either to break up the blockage or hook it so it can be pulled out. In this case, you don't want to push it in deeper. A coil-spring auger can be unwieldy; two people working

it (one on the handle, another on the crank) will find it easier.

- Note: The conventional flush toilet is a colossal water-waster. The tank holds five to seven gallons of water, and most people flush down thirty gallons daily. Of the water used in the average American residence, 45 percent goes for flushing. Most toilets were designed in the days before water shortages were a problem on our planet. There are simple ways to cut down on this squandering of water: Flush less, only when it's essential. Fill plastic containers with water and place them in the toilet tank to displace water permanently each time the tank refills. Don't use the toilet as an ashtray or wastebasket. Make sure it doesn't leak—it can waste more than fifty gallons a day. And if you ever have to replace a toilet, consider a water-saving toilet—there are 3½-gallon models available from the larger American manufacturers.

Septic Tanks

For those not hooked up to a municipal sewage system, there's the septic tank. Most are of precast concrete and have an access cover you should know the location of. Waste flows from the house into the septic tank where it settles, and bacterial action decomposes it. Over time a semisolid sludge collects at the bottom as liquid flows through an outlet into a drainage field. The tank's outlet is lower than the inlet to keep sewage from backing up into the house. The whole system—pipes, septic tank, and drainage field—are on an incline.

Septic tanks must be checked annually and cleaned every few years. Otherwise, the semisolid sludge at the bottom of the septic tank will get deep enough to put the tank out of commission. As a general rule, have the tank pumped out when the sludge is halfway up from the bottom of the tank to the surface of the liquid. (Septic tank cleaning companies will take care of this.) All tanks have a manhole or access cover. You should locate this right away so you can make periodic checks of the sludge level. Use a straight stick for measuring; the semisludge coats the stick, making its level easy to discern.

Other than checking and cleaning, there's little else necessary to keep a septic tank in good working order. Avoid excessive use of drain cleaners or high-foaming detergents (low- and nonfoaming detergents are fine), and don't connect discharge from gutters or swimming pools into it—too much water will flood it.

Cesspools

While a septic tank breaks down and treats sewage hygienically, cesspools are simply repositories that permit raw sewage to be leached into the ground. They are highly unsanitary and should be located well away from any underground source of water. They are also more prone than septic tanks to overflow caused by too much water running into them, by the surrounding soil being too wet to absorb any more liquid or by the surrounding soil becoming overly saturated with grease from the kitchen sink. Start thinking about converting to a septic tank system.

YOUR HEATING SYSTEM

How It Works

The basic operation of a nonelectric heating system is simple. It consists of four principal parts:

- the burner
- the furnace or boiler
- the heat distribution system
- the chimney

The burner generates heat by burning fuel. Part of the heat produced by burning the fuel is absorbed by the furnace or boiler and transferred to air or water, which in turn is distributed throughout the house by air ducts or by hot-water pipes and radiators. The heat not absorbed by the furnace or boiler is lost up the chimney in the process of disposing of smoke and gases.

An electric resistance heating system is the easiest to understand. It's also the most expensive to operate. Heat is generated either by electric heating cables spread throughout the house, or by an electric furnace and distributed throughout the house by hot-air ducts.

Heat pumps are combination electric heating and cooling systems that work on the same principle as an air-conditioner. (See page 174.) Heat is removed from one area and discharged into another. In summer heat is taken from house air and forced outdoors; in winter, the process is reversed—heat is extracted from the outside air and transferred inside. Even at very low temperatures air contains a certain amount of heat, though at temperatures below freezing, heat pumps often are boosted by an oil or gas burner or by a resistance-type electric heater.

A heat pump can be used in conjunction with a central air-conditioning unit. Some are incorporated together. The combination should be controlled by a thermostat sensitive enough that it will not turn on the full air-conditioning unit until the heat pump has done the preliminary cooling and then shut itself off.

Currently heat pumps are most effective in warmer states, but they are becoming more and more efficient. An electric heat pump can reduce an electric heating bill dramatically, and the rising cost of fossil fuels has made it a viable alternative to conventional oil-burning systems. A heat pump also is noiseless, clean, and doesn't require a flue or a chimney.

Is Your System Working Efficiently?

To ascertain this, you're going to have to call in a service technician. If the previous owner of the house was satisfied with the servicing, then it's to your advantage to call in the same serviceman familiar with your unit and go over these important checks.

- The carbon dioxide level: This measurement indicates the combustion efficiency of the system. Oil must be thoroughly mixed with air to burn completely. This usually requires more air than needed to convert the carbon and hydrogen in the fuel to carbon dioxide and water, which are the products of complete combustion. The amount of excess air can be determined by measuring the amount of carbon dioxide in the flue.

  Generally, the higher the carbon dioxide level, the less excess air used and the more efficient the combustion process. Too little air causes smoking, increases pollution, and reduces efficiency. A carbon dioxide level of 9 percent is considered good. Levels over 11 percent are excellent. If after tune-up and adjustment your technician cannot obtain a carbon dioxide reading of at least 9 percent without smoking, the furnace may be leaking air into the combustion chamber and need to be properly sealed, there may be too little or too much draft up the chimney, or the air and oil may not be thoroughly mixing for combustion. Correcting these problems requires modification or replacement of the burner.

- The flue gas temperature: The temperature of the flue gas leaving the furnace or boiler of an original furnace should be 400 to 600 degrees Fahrenheit (205 to 316 degrees Celsius) and of conversion burners 600 to 700 degrees Fahrenheit (316 to 371 degrees Celsius). Excessive temperatures often result from a malfunctioning burner nozzle (it's the nozzle that shoots a fine spray of oil droplets mixed with air into the furnace); otherwise the problem could be that the burner nozzle size is too large and more heat is being generated than can be utilized in the heat exchanger, or the heat exchanger surfaces may be badly sooted. Have them brushed and vacuumed.

- Soot buildup: Make sure the soot in the heat exchanger, firepot, and pipes is removed.

  Ask if your furnace has a fuel solenoid valve. These

electrically operated valves close off the fuel supply as soon as the fire has stopped. This prevents oil from dripping into the combustion chamber, which causes heavy smoke and soot deposits on the heat exchanger. If you don't have a fuel solenoid valve, it may pay to have one installed.

• Heating capacity: Make sure that your system isn't "oversized," meaning that it burns fuel so fast it switches on for only brief periods in all but the coldest weather. Such units are inefficient.

You can check for proper size on any very cold evening, when the system should run most of the time—at least forty minutes of every hour. If it runs less, its capacity should be reduced. A serviceman will determine if the unit is oversized through a series of measurements and calculations that take into account the average daily temperature, the amount of oil used, and alternative nozzle sizes. He may recommend that you go for a smaller nozzle; changing the burner nozzle usually can take up to 20 percent off the "size." With the smaller nozzle your system will run longer but burn less oil per unit of time, and the amount of heat loss up the chimney will be reduced. Note: If you carry out a major energy conservation improvement such as insulating or adding storm windows, it is particularly important to recheck furnace capacity, as these changes will make the heating plant oversized.

• Furnace fan: Have this checked. Possibly the on and off temperature settings of the furnace fan should be reset. To conserve fuel, the fan should continue to run to draw all the heat out of the burner and shut off when the furnace temperature is about 90 degrees Fahrenheit (32 degrees Celsius). It should not go on again until the burner comes on and raises the furnace temperature to about 110 degrees Fahrenheit (43 degrees Celsius).

• Chimneys or vents: Most produce more draft than necessary. Ask the serviceman to measure the draft both at the flue collar of the furnace and over the fire and to adjust the draft control if necessary.

A barometric draft damper can improve the efficiency of your system. Located on the pipe leading from the furnace to the chimney, it emits cool air to help with combustion while retaining warm air in the furnace. To do so, it has to open and shut freely.

- The burner: If your technician is unable to get an efficiency of 65 percent or better through a tune-up and nozzle-size adjustment, it may pay to get a new burner, which should increase efficiency to at least 75 to 80 percent.

  For older oil furnaces, as an alternative to replacing the whole unit, you might consider installing a flame retention burner in the existing unit. It should cut your heating bill by about 10 percent. On the market also are devices that reduce flue gas heat losses when the furnace is not operating, that recover heat from stack gas before it enters the chimney, and that lower boiler water temperatures when the outside temperature is mild.

Basic Maintenance

Of course, the best maintenance you can do is to have the furnace serviced in the summer. At that time heating contractors are always available and, if you need to replace or revamp your existing system, doing it in the summer will give you some time to think things through and shop around.

There are a few things you should keep tabs on throughout the winter.

- Air filters on forced-air furnaces, like those on air conditioners, must be cleaned at least once a month; otherwise air flow is impaired, less heat is transferred, and more fuel is used. A clogged filter will reduce heat output up to 70 percent. If a flashlight beam won't shine through the filter, clean it pronto! Usually a vacuum cleaner will do the job.

- Check the flame. If it's dirty or producing smoke, your burner needs an adjustment.

- Make sure the barometric damper swings freely (see page 169). If it sticks, oil it. While you're checking the damper, blow cigarette or candle smoke to see if it's sucked through and up the chimney. If it isn't, the chimney might be plugged. Have it checked.

If You Have a Natural-Gas Furnace

- Check that you're getting an even flame, without smoke. It should be blue, with no sign of yellow. If there is yellow, you can adjust the air setting yourself. Allow at least five minutes for the furnace to heat up before beginning. Open the vents and then shut them slowly, adjusting the yellow flame downward until it becomes blue and gives off no smoke.

- When the winter ends and you have no need of your furnace, be sure to have the pilot light, if there is one, extinguished for the summer (but don't blow it out). The pilot light consumes 10 percent of your annual gas supply. (See fig. 8-5.)

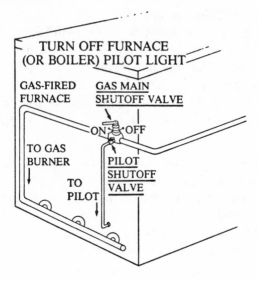

Fig. 8–5

If You Have a Warm-Air Heat Distribution System These use oil or natural gas for heat and electricity to operate a circulating fan. They draw cool air through registers in the floor, pass it over a firepot, then circulate it in ducts throughout the house.

• Lubricate the fan's motor at least two or three times during the winter season. Your instruction manual will tell you where and when.

• When you oil the motor, check the belt tension. There should be one-quarter to one-half-inch play midway between the pulleys. If there isn't, you're wasting electricity and wearing down a belt. There is a variable-diameter pulley on the motor that can be adjusted; try to set the belt so the fan will operate at its highest speed.

If You Have a Hot-Water System If a house isn't heated by circulating warm air, then it's usually heated by circulating hot water. Water has to be heated to 180 degrees Fahrenheit before it is pumped through baseboard radiators. Then it is returned to a burner for reheating. An expansion of heated water and a flow-control valve stops the circulation when the pump is not working. These systems operate on either oil or natural gas.

• When you turn on your system for the first time in the fall, bleed air trapped in each of the radiators. Normally, air will gradually accumulate in heating pipes, radiators, and baseboards. The early sign of this is a gurgling noise or the sound of running water every time the heat goes on. Air pockets will stop the water flow, and the radiators or baseboard units will stay cold.

— For radiators, with the heating system turned on, simply open the radiator's bleeder valve at one end to allow the excess air to escape. When a stream of water squirts out indicating that the air has been released, close the valve immediately. (Catch the hot water in a cup or rag.)

Repeat this process with each radiator. (See figs. 8-6 and 8-7.)

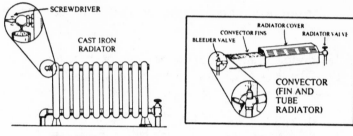

Fig. 8–6   **Fig. 8–7**

— For baseboard units, many have vent screws from which air can be drained. Otherwise, consult your boiler manual to see if it has a purge mechanism near the boiler that will allow you to release air from the system. Some baseboard systems run continuously around the house (instead of dead-ending in rooms), so the system must be purged at the boiler.

• The expansion tank has to have air space inside to facilitate the expansion of water. The relief valve that prevents excessive pressure buildups should also be checked periodically. Consult your owner's manual for specific maintenance instructions.

• Check the manufacturer's specifications to see if the water-level gauge on the boiler is marked at the proper level.

• An aquastat often controls the temperature of the water in your heating system and should be carefully adjusted to meet but not exceed hot-water requirements. Lowering an aquastat can save as much fuel as lowering a thermostat.

Note: Almost all modern aquastats have two separate settings—"lo" and "hi." They must always be set so that the high setting dial is at least 30 degrees Fahrenheit higher than the low. Failure to do this will give you hot water but no heat.

If You Have a Steam-Heat System While a hot-water heater circulates water at 180 degrees Fahrenheit through a house, a steam-heat system, usually found in older homes, boils water at 212 degrees Fahrenheit (boiling point). The steam produced then rises through pipes and distributes its heat from iron radiators. As the water cools, it condenses and flows naturally back down to the boiler for reheating. These systems usually are powered by an oil furnace.

- Flush out the system at least monthly. Open the flush valve and let the boiler drain until the water runs clear.

- Maintain the water in the boiler at the level recommended by the manufacturer. Too much water reduces the unit's efficiency; with too little, the unit won't operate.

- Feel the radiators to make sure they're giving off heat. If any are cold, check the air valves on the radiators or any vents on the steam main.

- Leaking radiator valves often can be repaired by tightening the packing nut (see fig. 8-8). If the leak persists, repair the radiator valve "packing" the same way an ordinary faucet is fixed (see pages 101–4).

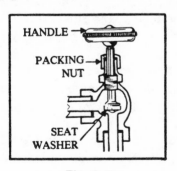

Fig. 8–8

If You Have Electric Heat Because there is no fuel combustion with the problems inherent in it, this is the one system that is practically maintenance-free, though it may be one of the most expensive to operate.

- Clean your heater periodically with a vacuum cleaner. Dust and dirt that accumulate on the coils can hinder efficiency and waste electricity.

- Many new homes are equipped with radiant heating coils running through ceilings and floors. Spot-check that the heat from these surfaces is even; otherwise you could have a broken cable, which is dangerous.

COOLING THE HOUSE

Air Conditioning

- How It Works

   An air-conditioner cools, dehumidifies, filters, and circulates air. Here's how:

   — Heated air is drawn from a room through a filter (removing dust) into an evaporator, where it is passed over heat exchange coils; its heat and moisture are absorbed by the coils. Then the conditioned air is blown back into the room by a fan or blower.

   — The copper cooling coils that absorbed the heat and moisture contain a cold (low-pressure) liquid refrigerant that turns to vapor when it absorbs the warm room air.

   — The now vaporized refrigerant takes the heat to a compressor, which compresses it even more, thereby increasing its temperature to a point higher than the outside air.

   — The next stop is a condenser. Inside the condenser, the hot (high-pressure) refrigerant is forced to liquify and give up the warm room air, which a fan discharges to the outside air.

   — A restrictor then reduces the pressure and temperature of the liquid refrigerant so it can return to the evaporator, take more heat out of the room air, and repeat the entire cycle.

- Maintaining Your Air Conditioner
  - Keep the filters clean or the unit will get clogged and more electricity will be required to turn the fan. The filter is located behind the removable front panel and can be vacuumed, washed, or shaken clean. Clean the filter at least once a month. When vacuuming, also vacuum any other accessible parts of the unit.
  - The blower and the electric motor should be lubricated. Follow the manufacturer's recommendations in your instruction manual.
  - Clogged condenser coils and fins (the metal grill or spines on the outside of the unit) can reduce a unit's efficiency. Again, consult your owner's manual for cleaning instructions.
  - In preparation for winter, remove the air-conditioner and seal the window. If that isn't possible, seal the unit on both sides to protect it from the weather and prevent it from letting cold air into the room. Air-conditioner covers are available from two to eight dollars at most home supply stores. They are made of tough plastic that you can secure around the outside of the unit. Be sure to measure your air-conditioner before you head out to buy a cover. (You can also use your own plastic and heavy tape.) Also see page 82.

Fans

Fans cost a fraction of the amount it costs to operate an air-conditioner, and the results can be quite pleasant. Keeping air moving, even if it's warm air, is the secret to staying comfortable in the summertime.

Ventilating Fans   These fans either bring air from the outside in or expel the air already inside the house (thereby creating suction, which brings in air from the outside). They're especially handy after sunset, when the air outside cools down much faster than the air inside. Window fans are the classic example.

Attic fans are the most effective of all. Permanently mounted in the ceiling at the top of a home, they suck air through windows and doors and blow it out enlarged vents in the attic. A large-enough attic fan can create a cool draft throughout a house. Large attic fans require professional installation. Nutone manufactures a small but powerful unit for smaller homes that fits between twenty-four-inch ceiling joists and can be installed by one person after an opening has been cut in the ceiling. Its louvers are also weather-stripped and close snugly when the fan is not running. This should be a feature of any fan you buy, or heat will escape in the winter.

Circulating Fans   These move air around a room, or around rooms within the house. They are most useful when the air inside a house is cooler than that outside (which can be accomplished by opening windows to receive the cool night air, then closing them in the morning).

Ceiling fans deserve their renewed popularity. They use no more electricity than a 15-watt light bulb, and they keep air moving throughout a room, unlike other circulating fans that tend to aim moving air wherever they're pointed. The result can be a 10- to 12-degree Fahrenheit reduction in room temperature. In winter they can cut a heating bill by as much as 20 percent; heated air rises, and the ceiling fan circulates it back downward, where it gets to you. Ceiling fans are especially good if you're stuck with cathedral ceilings and need to force down all the heat that's risen.

Portable fans are always handy to cool small areas, but they won't do much good unless they're of the oscillating variety.

HOME IMPROVEMENTS TO INCREASE THE EFFICIENCY OF YOUR COOLING OR HEATING SYSTEM

Power bills soar in the heat of summer or the dead of winter. Some northern utilities raise their rates between May 15 and

October 15 and lower them during the remaining seven-month billing period. Each additional degree of cooling can mean up to 5 percent more electricity used, and though extra degrees of heat cost less, it comes out to about the same because the temperature has to be raised so much. It's about the same in more temperate climates, just not as extreme. The following improvements to your home can drastically cut energy bills:

Insulation
Heat, like water, tends to seek its own level. In winter it escapes outside; in summer the flow is reversed and warm air tries to equalize with the cool air inside the house. All you can do is slow the flow, and insulation does it. Three inches of insulation in the ceiling can cut your fuel bill by 35 percent; two inches under the flooring can lop off 15 percent; two inches in the walls, another 10 percent . . . for a total of 60 percent. This alone should convince you it's worthwhile.

Thermostats
Replacing the existing thermostat with a clock thermostat can result in savings on the order of 10 to 15 percent. Ignoring any thermostat can result in a tremendous amount of waste. There are two times your wall thermostat should be set down: when you're asleep and when you're not at home. A single setback timer automatically lowers the temperature at night; a double one can lower the temperature for working people during the day as well.

Sealers
You may dismiss tiny escape outlets as inconsequential, but they aren't. A crack just one-eighth inch wide around an average door is as large as a hole in your wall about four by six inches—it's just like missing a window pane. On a windy day, up to 25 percent of your heat can be lost through windows and doors. Seal cracks with caulking or weather stripping.

- Caulking: This elastic, adhesive material is squeezed from a tube into gaps and seams where different types and sizes of materials meet, or where pipes and wires enter the house. It can be oil-based (which lasts one year) or acrylic latex (which lasts ten years) or silicone (which lasts twenty years and is the most pliable, capable of stretching with expansions and contractions of the materials it's sealing). Caulk also comes in many colors so it will blend in with the color of your house. Don't overlook any of the places in fig. 8-9, and see pages 134–39.

ALL THESE SHOULD BE CAULKED

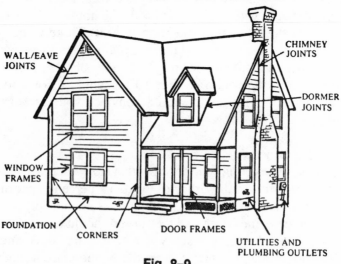

Fig. 8–9

- Weather stripping for doors: There are various types: plastic, foam, or spring metal that is squeezed by the door when it's closed is used on the top and sides (see fig. 8-10); there also are flexible plastic or rubber door sweeps that are attached to the bottom of the door with screws or nails, and threshold installations that are screwed into the floor (see fig. 8-11). Outside doors see a lot of action—the average door is opened and closed at least a thousand or more times per year—so the job should be done to last. Don't overlook the following doors: the garage door (the one you use for the car), any door leading into the house from a garage or porch, and a pull-down stairway leading into the attic (also insulate this one). Even mail chutes and large keyholes can leak a lot of expensive air, so seal or weather-strip them.

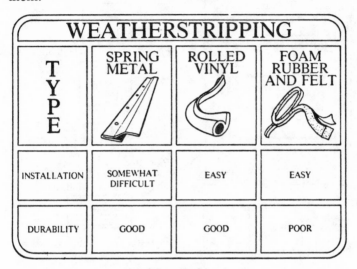

Fig. 8–10

Fig. 8–11

- Weather stripping for windows: Weather stripping comes in a variety of materials—metal and felt, spring metal, rubber and vinyl strips, adhesive foam, sponge rubber tape, and vinyl tubing (see fig. 8-12). When applying, pay special attention to windows facing west (these catch prevailing breezes) and windows facing north (these are exposed to coldest air in winter). If you have any windows that you never open, seal them permanently and install a permanent storm window on the inside or the outside. For windows you use, make sure the weather-stripping material allows the windows to slide open and shut freely while sealing it well when it's closed. Don't overlook the edges of window air-conditioners.

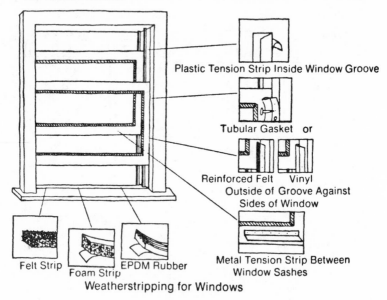

Plastic Tension Strip Inside Window Groove

Tubular Gasket **or**

Reinforced Felt   Vinyl
Outside of Groove Against
Sides of Window

Felt Strip

Foam Strip

EPDM Rubber

Metal Tension Strip Between
Window Sashes

Weatherstripping for Windows

Fig. 8–12

- Draft blockers: Compact, plastic foam cutouts that can be placed under electric switches or outlet plates. It has been estimated that as much as 8 percent of the heat lost in a typical home goes through the wall switches and sockets.

- Inside covers for kitchen exhaust fans: These are magnetically attached to seal the fan when it's not turned on. Most fans come with outside vent covers, but outside air can easily penetrate them, making an inside cover a necessity as well.

- Door and window draft guards: Thermal-lined, sausage-like tubes twenty-four to forty-four inches in length and two to three inches in diameter, filled with sand or some other loose insulating material. Also called doggle draft guards and draft dodgers, they're floppy and can be laid snugly against cracks to stop the flow of air. Excellent for doors and windows that cannot be sealed. If you like to open your window at night during the winter, place a draft guard at the base of the closed door to prevent heat loss in the rest of the house. When not in use, hang it on the doorknob.

Storm Windows, Shutters, and Shades

In winter and summer, window glass, which is only about one-eighth inch thick, needs insulation. Otherwise it acts as a conductor that works against a heating system or air-conditioner. Any of the following will work:

- Inside storm windows: Usually in kit form, these consist of plastic sheets to cover windows and some means of sealing and holding the sheets in place. The dead air trapped between the plastic and the window glass is an excellent insulator and stops the loss of heat. These kits all do the same thing, but prices vary greatly, according to the thickness of the plastic sheets and the way they are attached to the window frame.

- Outside storm windows: These perform the same function as those installed inside; the difference is that outside windows are permanently attached and need not be removed during the warm months. Most models have three tracks—one for a screen and two for upper and lower panes of glass. Shop around! Cheaper versions don't have rigid frames and won't fit closely against the window frame. Others don't have weather stripping throughout or tight-fitting sashes that lock firmly in position and sit closely together in the tracks to ensure air-tightness. Beyond this, make sure there are two small "weepholes" about one-eighth inch in diameter at the bottom to allow rainwater that penetrates the screen to run from the windowsill. (See fig. 8-13.)

TYPES OF STORM WINDOWS
FOR DOUBLE HUNG WINDOWS

Fig. 8–13

Note: The old version is the removable single-pane storm window that is replaced in summer with a screen. These work admirably, though they are trouble to put up and take down. For those with second-story bedrooms and who want to sleep alfresco, there is an insect-free grace period of a week or two between the time the storms come down and the screens go up.

• Shutters and shades: In summer, the object is to keep out sunlight that will work against the air conditioning. In winter, to work really well, window shades and shutters have to be closed manually when the sun goes down to prevent heat loss from the house, and they must be open when the sun comes up to receive the sun's radiant energy. (Storm windows—inside or out—perform both functions, preventing heat loss and absorbing winter sunlight.)

Air Deflectors for Registers or Vents (See Fig. 8-14)

They allow you to direct heated or cooled air into a room for maximum temperature control and energy savings. Often vents are inefficiently placed, and misdirected air can end up blowing heat or air conditioning against the ceiling or behind drapes or a piece of furniture. Deflectors are simple, adjustable metal or plastic devices that magnetically snap onto any vent.

Fig. 8-14

Heat Reflectors for Radiators

Radiators are located against walls—usually outside walls—all of which receive an unnecessary share of the heat. A heat reflector placed behind a radiator reflects radiant heat back into the room, where it belongs. Composed of rigid plastic foam covered on one side with metal foil, the foam insulates, and the foil (positioned toward the room) reflects heat.

Sprayer Units for Air-Conditioners

An innovation in holding down air-conditioning costs is installing a water sprayer unit in front of the outdoor compressor. Because the spray holds down the temperature inside the unit, the condenser runs less because it "thinks" the temperature is cooler than it really is. This kind of precooling can cut electric bills by 20 percent a year.

For Fireplaces

A fireplace is likely to steal more heat than it delivers; the draft up the chimney draws warmth from the room along with warmth from the fire. Heat loss is quite high as a fire dies down, and a fireplace with a flue damper that doesn't function properly can let expensive heat escape up the chimney during the entire heating season. In winter the damper should remain closed unless a fire is burning. In summertime it can be left open to serve as a vent unless you're using air conditioning. (See fig. 8-15.)

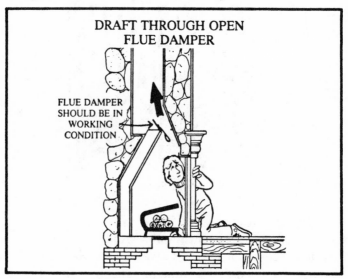

DRAFT THROUGH OPEN
FLUE DAMPER

FLUE DAMPER
SHOULD BE IN
WORKING
CONDITION

Fig. 8–15

Several devices that can be employed to give you both the pleasure and the efficiency you ought to be getting from your fireplace:

- Glass door fire screens: Like sunlight passing through a windowpane, radiant energy from a fire passes through closed glass doors and warms the room. Adjustable vents or dampers at the bottom keep the draw of room heat to a minimum. When you leave the room, the dampers can be closed completely, thus preventing cold outside air from coming in.

- Hollow-tube grates: Combining glass doors with a tubular grate makes for the most efficient fireplace you can own. Such a grate is used in place of andirons and is composed of a set of C-shaped pipes whose open ends face into the room near floor level. Logs rest on the tubes, which curve up the back of the firebox and back over the logs to face into the room. The heat from the fire creates a draft—cool air enters the tubes on the bottom, is heated, and emerges at the top. Some models, such as that shown in fig. 8-16, use an electric motor to increase circulation.

FIREPLACE CONVECTION PIPES

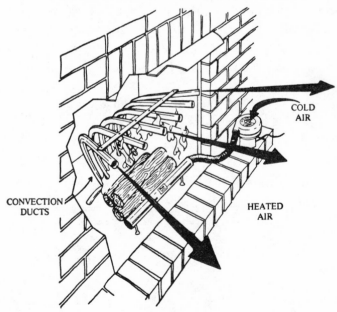

Fig. 8-16

- Fire board: Any piece of solid material such as Masonite or fireproof board can be used to cover the fireplace and stop the flow of warm air up the chimney once the fire gets low.

Also on the market are fireproof canvas curtains that can be drawn over the front of the fireplace, but check just how fireproof these are before using them.

- Chimney top damper: Ideal for old houses without fireplace dampers, or even for new houses whose dampers have become warped by intense heat. Installed outside, on the top of the chimney, this cast-aluminum damper protects against heat loss and keeps out birds, squirrels, rain, and snow. Furthermore, because warm air remains inside the chimney when it's closed, your fireplace will draw immediately rather than smoking when you start a fire.

- When using a fireplace without glass doors, close the doors to the room. Otherwise the draft caused by the fire will pull heated air from other rooms and up the chimney. If there are no doors you can close, turn the furnace thermostat down to 52 degrees Fahrenheit so the furnace won't be producing even more hot air to be drawn up the chimney.

- An unused fireplace should be sealed off, preferably with a board across the front (see fig. 8-17). If you like the look

SEALING UNUSED FIREPLACES
WITH PLYWOOD BOARD & CAULKING

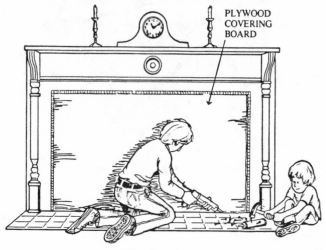

PLYWOOD COVERING BOARD

Fig. 8–17

of an open fireplace, the chimney can be sealed (see fig. 8-18) and the flue closed. A sealed chimney prevents drafts within the chimney, protects against rain and snow, and keeps unwanted squirrels and birds from moving in.

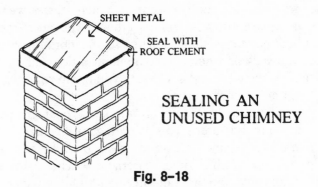

SHEET METAL

SEAL WITH
ROOF CEMENT

SEALING AN UNUSED CHIMNEY

Fig. 8–18

THE ROOF OVER YOUR HEAD

The roof is the most taken-for-granted part of the house—until it starts leaking right next to your baby grand piano or stereo system. Roofs come in all shapes and sizes, but they have one thing in common: They are unsafe places to work. Here are three safety rules:

- Wear soft-soled shoes to prevent slipping and damage to the roof.
- Never work on a wet roof, for it might be slippery.
- When inspecting or working on a roof with a steep pitch, for support toss a rope over the ridge and fasten it to a window frame, tree, or other solid object on the other side of the house.

Roof Construction

The underpinnings of most residential roofs consist of rafters or, in the case of flat roofs, roof joists spaced about sixteen inches apart. Many newer houses have truss roofs. A truss is a large preconstructed frame that serves as both a roof rafter and a ceiling joist. Usually they are shaped like giant triangles crisscrossed with supporting pieces of timber. The long, hypotenuse side is the joist (to which the ceilings are attached), and the top, slanting timbers are the rafters (to which the roof is attached). The same principle is used on older homes with slanting roofs, except that their trusses were assembled in place instead of on the ground. For our purposes, remember that the ceiling attaches to the bottom of joists (which you walk on when you go up in the attic), and the roof is secured to the top of rafters (which you bump your head on when you go up in the attic).

A sheathing, usually made of plywood, fiberboard, or planking, is nailed to the rafters. This sheathing is called a roof deck and, like that covering the exterior walls, provides a smooth, continuous base to which other material is attached. Most roof decks are covered with asphalt-saturated building paper, and then shingles or tiles go on top of that.

Homeowners can extend the life of their roof, especially old asphalt shingle roofs, by having them coated with any of several special compounds made for this purpose. These coatings also can be used to change the color of the roof for those who want a change. When the roof is replaced, it is better to lay new shingles atop the old ones. This makes the roof tighter and can reduce the cost considerably.

Roof Leaks

The easiest way to find where the roof is leaking is to head up to the attic right away. If it's still raining, take a bucket along to catch water and prevent further damage. If the attic isn't properly illuminated, you'll also need a flashlight.

If you have a flat roof you probably don't have an attic, but chances are the roof is leaking right above the drip in the ceiling. If you have a pitched roof, water could be entering uphill, running along a joist for a few feet, and then dripping down. Find the leak with a flashlight. Mark the spot by either driving a long nail or pushing a wire through the hole so you will be able to find it when you're outside on the roof. You can also temporarily stop a leak by applying a sealer or caulking compound to the hole. If you're fortunate, the cause of the leak is a loose or torn shingle that can be glued down with asphalt roofing cement, then nailed with broad-headed, galvanized nails. (Once you've driven the nails in, always remember to apply asphalt cement to the nailheads, because water can leak in around the heads.)

The virgin homeowner shouldn't have too much trouble making minor repairs to a roof covered with asphalt or wood shingles or to flat roofs covered with roof felt. However, it's best to leave slate, tile, and asbestos shingle repairs to an expert. These roofing materials are brittle and can even be damaged by walking on them, not to mention by your attempts to repair them.

Ice Dams
Each winter ice dams cause millions of dollars in damage to homes. They are formed when attic heat moves upward to warm the roof and melts roof snow. The water runs downward to the edge of the roof where colder conditions exist and the water refreezes, thus forming an ice dam. As snow continues to melt and the water runs downward, the ice dam stops it and it eventually backs up under the shingles and flows into the house, damaging insulation, ceilings, or wall cavities. Take precautions if you see them start to form, or if the previous owner has told you that there's a problem.

How to Prevent Them Though a number of factors enter into the formation of ice dams, the fundamental problem is undesirable attic heat, which results in a warm roof surface. The logical solution is to try to maintain a cold roof. This can be done by insulating roof ceilings far more than customary to minimize heat losses and attic temperatures, and by ventilating profusely at all eaves and ridge for a natural flow of air to sweep out the warmed attic air. See fig. 8-19; the arrows show movement of air when there is adequate insulation and ventilation.

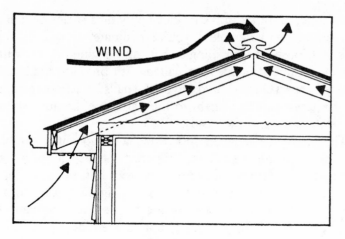

Fig. 8–19

To prevent seepage into the house (but not ice dams), a flashing strip (see the next section) can be installed along each eave. The bottom edge should overhang the edge by at least a quarter inch. The upper edge should extend up the roof far enough to cover a point at least one foot inside the interior wall line.

Some homeowners install electric cables zigzagging along the eaves and in the valleys to prevent ice dams. Unfortunately, the melting effectiveness of such heat tapes is limited to only a few inches from the cable, and the sawtooth melting often causes uproof secondary ice dams to develop. In addition, these electric cables use up a great deal of energy.

As a last resort, most snow can be removed with a roof rake and a push broom. However, extreme caution must be taken to ensure personal safety and cause as little damage to the roof as possible. Never chop through the ice down to the shingles or use a blowtorch.

Roof Flashing

The most vulnerable points on any roof are where two roof angles come together and form a valley, where a roof joins a vertical surface such as a chimney, or where a porch or shed roof meets an outside wall. These joints usually are made tight with metal flashing, which can be copper, aluminum, or galvanized iron.

If a leak occurs around valley flashing and you can't locate a hole, it's safe to assume that water is getting under the flashing by running up under the shingles that partially cover the flashing and then seeping under it. If you've got an asphalt shingle roof, lift up the ends of the shingles and work roofing cement under them to bond the shingles to the flashing. About all you can do with wood, asbestos, and other rigid shingles is to apply roofing cement carefully along the shingle ends to create a tight seal with the flashing.

Chimney flashing runs under the roof shingles and then comes up the chimney sides. The lower part is called base flashing; the upper vertical part, counterflashing. The ends of the counterflashing are bent at a right angle so they can be slipped into the joints of the chimney and be held in place by mortar. If they pull out, clean out loose mortar, force the flashing back into the joint, and pack in fresh mortar. Because flashing around chimneys is made of more than one piece of metal, leaks can occur between them. Here the best remedy (short of hiring an expert) is to give all the flashing a liberal coating of roofing cement.

The intersections of walls and roofs are flashed similarly to chimneys, except the counterflashing is omitted since the base flashing is turned up under the siding or other wall covering. If the flashing is faulty, coat the juncture with roofing cement. If this doesn't seal it, both the siding and the shingles must be removed along the joint. Time to call a roofer.

WOOD DECAY

If allowed to spread, wood decay will destroy your home. Minute plants called fungi cause it. Like all living things, fungi need water, almost always more than is present in the air. When wood in a house or other structure becomes damp, the ever-present fungus spores come to life and use the wood as food. Drying sends the plants back into dormancy until the next period of wetness.

Occasionally decay is found to extend many feet from the nearest possible source of moisture. This is likely caused by water-conducting fungi that commonly produce rootlike strands to the moisture's source. Trace the fungi to their source of moisture (usually the ground) and cut off the connection.

The signs that moisture is not under control in your house are:

- rust stains appear around nailheads
- paint peels and blisters
- paint discolors at joints
- siding swells and buckles
- window sashes are discolored or decayed
- dark stains develop from moisture seeping out from under siding

Causes of Serious Decay and What Can Be Done to Prevent It

- Undrained soil around the house: Moist building sites should be well drained. The soil surface should slope away from the house. Downspouts should discharge into drains or masonry gutters or onto splash blocks that lead the water several feet away from the house. Dense shrubbery or vines planted too close to the house also can interfere with drainage and air movement and thereby enable fungi to grow.

- Improper ventilation in crawl space under basementless houses: Under houses without cemented basements, the soil supplies moisture vapor to the air. In winter this may condense on the cold sills and joist ends, just as the moisture of the air condenses on the outside of a glassful of ice water. This sweating, if continued, wets the wood to the point where decay fungi can attack it. There are two ways to prevent this: (1) Provide cross ventilation for all parts of the crawl space by openings in the foundation or skirting (what skirts the house along the ground) on opposite sides of the buildings, best near the corners. (2) Place a vapor-resistant cover over the ground in the crawl space. This stops at its source the moisture vapor that causes the sweating and makes it possible to use smaller vents or to close most or all of the vents during the cold weather without bringing on decay.

- Wood such as grade stakes, concrete forms, or stumps left on or in soil under houses as well as soil, trash, firewood, or lumber piled against walls or sills: Remove it.

- Leaks around bathtub/shower combinations, kitchen fixtures, and laundry rooms: These are high-priority caulking jobs. Don't put them off.

- Wood parts of the house in direct contact with the soil, especially porches with dirt fills under concrete or masonry: If the house has a wood porch or steps, the obviously decayed boards or bases of pillars should be replaced with treated or naturally durable wood. Allow no wood to be in contact with the soil unless the wood is thoroughly impregnated with a suitable preservative. For the greatest safety there should be no wood-soil contact of any kind.

- Wood parts embedded in masonry near the ground: Localized decay in joints and bases of uprights may be arrested by flooding treatments with water-repellent preservatives. Lower ends of stair carriages or stringers on bricks, stone, or concrete should be raised well above ground level.

- Use of unseasoned and infected lumber: Make sure wood can dry out.

- Roof decay due to rain leaks and improper flashing: Repair. See the preceding section.

- Unventilated attics: See pages 189–90, fig. 8–19 for more about attic ventilation.

- Winter moisture condensing on the inside of window glass and running down into the wood: Outfitting your home with storm windows can greatly reduce this condensation as well as save a great deal of money on heating.

- Cold pipes that "sweat" and moisten adjacent to wood for long periods: Where the water supply enters the house at a temperature as low as 50 degrees Fahrenheit, there may be enough condensation of moisture on concealed pipes in walls and floors to cause decay. Where the pipes are exposed, insulate them.

- Roofs without overhang or gutters that let too much rainwater run over the siding: Leaks in cornices, gutters, or downspouts can lead to decay in the walls below them. Remedy them. (See pages 142–48.)

TERMITES

Termites feed on cellulose in wood, and because they work from beneath and from within, they often are not discovered until pressure collapses the wood they've hollowed out. Like bees and ants, termites live in a highly organized society. There are three caste groups: kings and queens, soldiers to guard the colony, and workers to eat up your house. At certain times of the year the "reproductives"—the young kings and queens—swarm out of their nests to form new colonies. If you see any (they look like flying ants), you're in trouble. Another bad sign is finding the wings they shed before they mate.

Termite colonies nest in warm, moist soil and maintain contact with wood through the workers, which are pale, soft-bodied, and wingless. Damp wood in contact with the ground is the easiest target, and they also may build earthen tunnels made of wet dirt from the ground up to wood.

Because the chemicals needed to control termites are toxic to animals and plant life and because there also is danger of contaminating the water supply, it's best to call in a professional to take care of your termite problem.

Termite Patrol

Check for termites at least annually, and call an exterminator if you see them flying around or locate any on the following search.

- Look for earthen tunnels in the following locations:
  — along masonry foundation and basement walls
  — around openings where pipes enter walls
  — along the surface of metal pipes
- Examine all cracks in slabs and loose mortar in masonry walls. Check all joints where wood meets with concrete or masonry, at walls, slabs, piers, etc.
- Inspect all wood and wood structures that are near the ground. Pay special attention to any that touch the house, such as fences, wood trellises, carports, etc. Examine crawl spaces that provide moist conditions.
- Check windowsills, door thresholds, porches, and the underside of stairs. Look for peeling and blistering paint, a sure sign of moisture.
- If you suspect that wood has termite damage, probe with a sharp point, such as an ice pick or penknife. If the point penetrates the wood to a depth of one-half inch when you use only hand pressure, it's a good indication of wood damage by termites.

Chapter 9

THE LAY OF THE LAND

The virgin homeowner can inherit anything from a scraggly bit of lawn to the most well-manicured acreage. In either case —and everything in between—the homeowner is going to have to put in some time in the yard either maintaining or improving it.

ABOUT LANDSCAPING

The design of a yard should be as carefully considered as that of a house. Too often an inexperienced gardener will be driving past a nursery, see some marigolds or daffodils blooming

196

out front, pull in, and do some heavy impulse shopping. He or she drives home—self-congratulatory—and digs some circles and squares in the yard for the new flora. The results rarely complement the house and grounds.

Good landscaping is mainly applying good common sense. If you determine the uses to which various areas around the home will be put, this will not only determine the sizes of the areas involved and the traffic patterns needed to serve them but also will dictate part of the yard design.

The plants you choose will then enable you to carry out these schemes. It's important that you select plant material that does well in your area. The plantings in your yard are supposed to improve each year, not die out! Don't expect a tree from a Georgia mail-order nursery to do well in New Hampshire.

Plants are used for several things:

- to define activity areas
- to delineate traffic patterns
- to screen or protect
- to shade
- to enhance

Illustration 9-1 gives an idea of the shapes and sizes available to you.

A Few Landscaping Rules

- Use trees and shrubs to provide a gradual transition between the abrupt vertical lines of the house and the horizontal line of the ground.
- Design the job as a whole, even if you only intend to landscape bits at a time. Mark areas to be planted with wooden stakes and string (or whitewash or old paint) and live with them awhile before you start digging.
- Except for large shade trees or accent shrubs, most plants look best in groupings of three or more.

EVERGREEN

CONIFERS

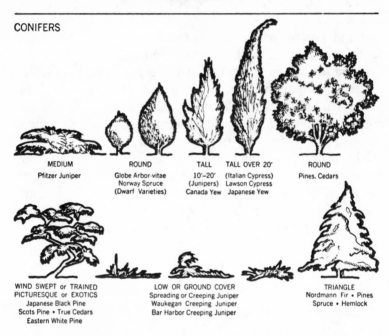

MEDIUM	ROUND	TALL	TALL OVER 20'	ROUND
Pfitzer Juniper	Globe Arbor-vitae Norway Spruce (Dwarf Varieties)	10'–20' (Junipers) Canada Yew	(Italian Cypress) Lawson Cypress Japanese Yew	Pines, Cedars

WIND SWEPT or TRAINED PICTURESQUE or EXOTICS
Japanese Black Pine
Scots Pine • True Cedars
Eastern White Pine

LOW OR GROUND COVER
Spreading or Creeping Juniper
Waukegan Creeping Juniper
Bar Harbor Creeping Juniper

TRIANGLE
Nordmann Fir • Pines
Spruce • Hemlock

BROADLEAF EVERGREENS

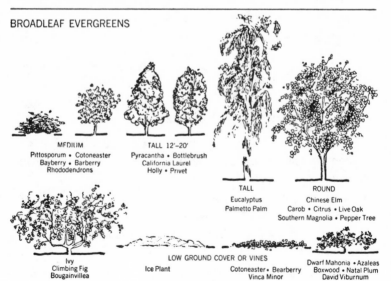

MEDIUM
Pittosporum • Cotoneaster
Bayberry • Barberry
Rhododendrons

TALL 12'–20'
Pyracantha • Bottlebrush
California Laurel
Holly • Privet

TALL
Eucalyptus
Palmetto Palm

ROUND
Chinese Elm
Carob • Citrus • Live Oak
Southern Magnolia • Pepper Tree

Ivy
Climbing Fig
Bougainvillea

LOW GROUND COVER OR VINES
Ice Plant

Cotoneaster • Bearberry
Vinca Minor

Dwarf Mahonia • Azaleas
Boxwood • Natal Plum
David Viburnum

Fig. 9–1

DECIDUOUS

TREES

ROUND—GLOBE—SHAPED
Arnold Crabapple • Japanese Maple
Mulberry • Green Ash • Pistachio
Hawthorne Sycamore

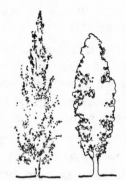

FASTIGIATE TREE OR COLUMNAR TREE
Dawyck Beech • Siberian Crabapple
English Oak • Poplar • Sargent Cherry
Sentry Ginkgo • Lombardy Poplar
Pyramidal European Birch
Linden

BROAD OVAL TREE
Bradford Pear
Sugar Maple • Laburnum
European Mountain Ash

FAN SHAPED—HORIZONTAL BRANCHING
Flowering Dogwood
Silk Tree • Redbud
Amur Maple

CONICAL TREE OR TRIANGLE
American Sweetgum
Pin Oak

SHRUBS

LOW 1½'–5'
February Daphne • Bush Cinquefoil
Anthony Waterer Spirea
Japanese Barberry

MEDIUM 5'–12'
Snowball • Forsythia • English Privet

TALL 12'–18'
Crapemyrtle • Spindle Tree
Russian Olive • Lilac

LOW, GROUND COVER OR VINES

Prostrate Pyracantha

Lantana

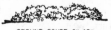

GROUND COVER 6"–18"
Cranberry Cotoneaster
Carpet Bugle • Memorial Rose
Aaronsbeard St. Johnswort

VINES
Wisteria • Passionflower • Bittersweet
Virginia Creeper • Clematis • Grapes

- Harmony is important. Choose plants that complement each other and relate their mature size to the size of your house. A general rule is to use low plantings for a one-story house, taller for a two-story. Shrubbery below windows should never grow above the sills.

- Corner plantings should compensate for the sharp vertical angle of the house and the open space beyond. Trees and shrubs that will grow higher than the eaves work well here. Also, extending the plantings beyond the corner gives the appearance of greater width.

- The front entrance should be emphasized by a plant grouping or a large, unusual plant. Potted trees and shrubs are good on large porches or entrance areas.

Landscaping to Save Money and Energy

The major part of your energy bill goes to heat the house in the winter; for homeowners with air conditioning, cooling can cost almost as much as heating. These two illustrations show how trees and earth can be used to fullest advantage in winter (see fig. 9-2) and in summer (see fig. 9-3).

LANDSCAPE TECHNIQUES: USING TREES
AND EARTH TO BEST ADVANTAGE

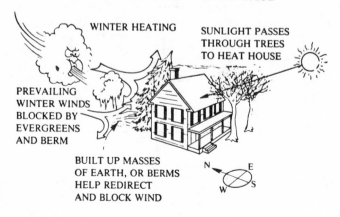

Fig. 9–2

LANDSCAPE TECHNIQUES: USING TREES
AND EARTH TO BEST ADVANTAGE

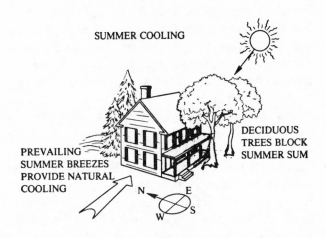

Fig. 9–3

Depending on where you live, the basic premises behind landscaping to save energy are as follows:

- Cold climates
  — Concentrate plantings on the north, east, and west sides of the house to protect against wind, the worst heat robber. Plant rows of trees and shrubs to provide deep, thick windbreaks.
  — Put a patio or pavement on the south side of the house. These absorb the sun's energy and extend the outdoor season by a few weeks.
  — Keep a wide swath of the property from the southeast to the southwest free of trees and shrubs. This lets through even the low winter sun, maximizing its energy donation.
  — To control summer heat, plant a tall, high-crowned tree close to the south wall of the house. When the tree is mature, it will shade the roof without interfering with warming southern sun in the winter.

- Hot, arid climates
  - Concentrate your gardening indoors. Houseplants improve the indoor climate by humidifying and cooling the air, lessening the need for air conditioning.
  - Put low shrubs such as mesquite or cactus on the east side. They absorb heat without blocking the light.
  - Protect the western exposure with a low, densely leafed tree, high bushes, or low cactus. These absorb heat and cut down on glare.
  - Protect the western side of your landscaping with lots of mulch (wood chips are very good) interspersed with plants. This cuts down on glare and conserves moisture.
  - Patios or balconies are best on the northern or eastern sides, to minimize heat storage.
  - If your budget is limited, concentrate your resources on blocking the sun on the southern side of the house. Tall trees such as the desert gum, and thickly vined trellises are very effective sun screens.

- Hot, humid climates
  - Your goals in this kind of climate are to cut down on heat storage and maximize ventilation. Avoid pavement in your landscaping, and use palm trees to create a high, airy canopy over the house.
  - Protect the southern exposure with trellises and vines, especially deciduous vines, which lose their leaves and let in winter sun.
  - Funnel the prevailing breezes with plantings of trees and bushes. Fragrant flower trees are an especially well-planned choice, since they scent the cooling air when they are in bloom.
  - If resources are limited, concentrate on protecting the southern side of the house from the midday sun.

- Temperate climates
  - Your goals in this kind of climate are to protect the northern exposure from winter winds and the southern exposure from summer heat.
  - Plant small to medium-size flowering trees at the south-

western and northeastern exposures to cut down on exposure to wind and sun.

— Protect the northern and western walls with a thick evergreen hedge.

— A patio and trellis on the southern side provides shade in the summer and an effective heat collector in early spring and late fall. A single row of deciduous trees and low hedges adds to these effects.

— Create a wind wall on the northern side to shield against winter storms. Work away from the house, starting with a row of tall, thick evergreens. Dense, deciduous trees and bushes should be planted to the north of the evergreens to add to their effect.

LAWNS

The four basic maintenance tips for a successful lawn are:

- Plant a grass type and variety that is specifically adapted to your area.

- Mow at proper height on a steady basis. Don't let grass grow too long and then smother it with cuttings or shock it with a heavy mowing. Keeping the grass cut also provokes deeper root growth.

- Fertilize at recommended rates and on a schedule that fits the growth cycle of your cool- or warm-season grass.

- Water deeply and infrequently, and only when the lawn needs it. This will promote deep root growth.

Grasses
All lawn grasses can be divided into two categories:

- Warm-season grasses
  - best adapted to the southern United States
  - do their growing in the late spring, summer, and early fall
  - go dormant and turn brown when cold weather comes
  - established from sprigs (runners or individual plants), plugs (round cores of grass and sod), and sod

EASY REGIONAL LAWN CARE

	NORTH-EAST	SOUTH-EAST	SOUTH-WEST	NORTH-WEST
January/February	• If lawn isn't under a layer of snow, treat any snowmold present with a fungicide spray.	• Apply pre-emergent weed killer. • Fertilize Bermuda-, bahia-, St. Augustine- and zoysiagrass. • On fertilized grass, apply a multi-purpose insecticide against grubs.	• Dethatch. • Begin planting new grass and fertilizing. • Apply pre-emergent herbicides against crabgrass, bluegrass.	• Treat snowmold if present.
March/April	• Dethatch. • Begin planting new grass or patching old and fertilizing. **Apply:** • Pre-emergent herbicide against crabgrass • Multi-purpose weed killer • Multi-purpose diazinon insecticide against emergence of grubs.	• Repair winter damage with sod, plugs, patches or seed. **Feed:** • Centipede-grass with nitrogen • Cool-season grasses if not fed last fall. • Give lawn a low mowing.	• Fertilize warm-season grasses at first indication of growth. • Overseed if necessary. • Apply multi-purpose weed killer to broadleaf weeds. • Give lawn a low mowing.	• Dethatch. • Plant cool-season grasses. • Spotseed if necessary. • Fertilize cool-season grasses. **Apply:** • Pre-emergent herbicide • Multi-purpose weed killer to broadleaf weeds. • Give lawn low mowing.
May	• Feed (wait till Bermuda- and zoysiagrass start to green). • Plant new zoysia- and Bermudagrass. • Give grass a low mowing.	• Dethatch. • Plant warm-season grasses. • Feed warm-season grasses except centipede. • Apply multi-purpose weed killer.	• Plant Bermudagrass. **Apply:** • Herbicides to warm-season grasses to kill crabgrass • Multi-purpose weed killer to broadleaf weeds.	• Repeat fertilization of cool-season grasses. • Re-apply multi-purpose weed killer to broadleaf weeds, if needed.

	NORTH-EAST	SOUTH-EAST	SOUTH-WEST	NORTH-WEST
June	**If needed, repeat:** • Application of multi-purpose weed killer • Multi-purpose insecticide.	**Apply:** • Multi-purpose insecticide • Herbicides.	• Apply a multi-purpose diazinon insecticide. • Raise mowing height to protect grass from scorching.	**If needed, repeat:** • Application of herbicide against crabgrass. • Multi-purpose insecticide.
July/August	• Water generously but infrequently. • Spot-treat crabgrass. • Re-apply multi-purpose insecticide. • Raise mowing height to prevent lawn scorching.	• Water generously but infrequently. • Raise mowing height to prevent lawn scorching. • Continue thorough maintenance program to prevent brown patch.	• If needed, apply multi-purpose insecticide. • Water generously but infrequently.	• Apply multi-purpose insecticide. • Water generously but infrequently (especially cool-season grasses). • Raise mowing height to prevent lawn from scorching.
September	• Fertilize and lime. • Re-apply multi-purpose weed killer. • Put in new lawn or patch old one. • Dethatch.	• Apply pre-emergent herbicide against annual bluegrass. • Fertilize. • Plant cool-season grasses.	• Fertilize warm-season grasses. • Dethatch. • Apply pre-emergent herbicide against annual bluegrass, if present.	• Fertilize cool-season grasses. • Dethatch. • Apply pre-emergent herbicide against annual bluegrass.
October/November	• Spray to control snowmold if it was present last spring. • Keep lawn mowed until growth stops.	• Apply multi-purpose weed killer to broadleaf weeds. • Overseed. • Fertilize for last time.	• Overseed with cool-season grasses. • Apply multi-purpose weed killer to broadleaf weeds. • Final feeding.	• Reseed or spot seed. • Final feeding and mowing. • Treat snowmold if disease was present last spring.

Courtesy of Spectrum Home and Garden Products

— most popular types are bahia, Bermuda, centipede, St. Augustine, and zoysia

• Cool-season grasses
  — best adapted to northern climates

— do their growing in cool weather of spring and fall
— growth slows down in summer, and they go dormant in winter
— established by seeding
— most common types are Kentucky bluegrass, fescue, bent grass, and ryegrass

Mowing

- A lawn that is mowed when necessary and at the right height can better resist invasions of weeds, insects, and disease. Here are the recommended heights for the most common grasses in the United States:

Grass	*Height (inches)*
Bahia grass	2–3
Bent grass	¼–1
Bermuda grass	
Common	½–1½
Hybrid	½–1
Bluegrass	
Common	2–3
Improved (varies by variety)	¾–2½
Buffalo grass	1–3
Carpet grass	1–2
Centipede grass	1–2
Dichondra	½–1½
Fescue	
Chewing	1–2
Red	2–3
Tall	3–4
Annual ryegrass	1½–2
Perennial ryegrass	1–2½
St. Augustine grass	1–2½
Zoysia grass	½–1½

- Warm-season grasses generally are trimmed shorter than cool-season grasses. Close mowing in summer, however, can allow warm-season grasses to scorch and weaken them severely. Increase the height of the cut in summer as temperatures increase and reduce it as temperatures fall.
- If you've let the yard go, cut no more than half the growth.
- Sharp turns can cause uneven cutting.
- Alternate mowing patterns. Otherwise soil is compacted and wear patterns begin to show in the yard.
- If the lawn is wet—wait! Not only can it cause uneven mowing, but also the clippings can mat and suffocate the grass.

Lawn Mower Maintenance

- Sharpen the blades with a file whenever they get dull—this is important.
- Keep motor oil at proper level (see your instructions).
- Clean the mower after using it.
- When storing the mower for the winter, clean it and drain the gasoline tank. In the spring, refill the tank, clean the spark plug, and change the oil.

Mowing Safety Checklist

Before mowing:
- Put on close-fitting and sturdy, nonslip shoes.
- Go over the lawn carefully to pick up stones, wire, toys, dog bones—anything the mower might pick up and sling.
- Know where any hard, solid obstacles might be hidden in the grass.
- Add fuel and wipe up spills before starting the mower. Always pour gasoline outdoors and store it away from flames, sparks, or other ignition sources. Keep it in an approved safety container.

- If your electric mower isn't labeled "double insulated," *never* plug it into anything but a grounded (three-prong) outlet.
- Adjust the cutting height before starting the mower.
- Read through the mower instruction book again, especially if it's been a while since you last used the mower.

While you mow:

- Always start up outdoors, near the lawn you're going to mow.
- Never run the mower over gravel, stones, or hard, immovable objects such as pipes, rocks, or sidewalk edges.
- Mow forward as much as possible, so you can see where you're going.
- Go across slopes with walk-behind mowers; go up or down with riding mowers.
- Keep the electric mower cord out of the cutting path.
- Stay clear of the blade housing edge and the discharge chute.
- Never point the discharge chute at others.
- Turn off the mower if you leave it even for a moment.

And be sure to:

- Disconnect the spark plug or power cord before working on your mower.
- Have safety devices in their proper position.
- Let an expert periodically examine your mower for leaks, electrical shorts, blade condition, and balance.
- Treat gasoline like the high explosive it really is.
- Keep the power cord of an electric mower in near-new condition.

When riding mower, be sure to:
- Look back before you back up.
- Keep kids away from (and off of) the mower.

Watering

- Going easy on the watering deepens root growth, which makes for healthier grass. Don't get upset if the lawn browns in summer. Most grasses have good tolerance to drought and usually will recover when fall rains begin.

- Thirsty lawns take on a blue-green color that usually shows first under trees where roots compete with grass for moisture. And if your footprints leave impressions that don't immediately spring back, that's another indication that the lawn could use water.

- Watering lightly too often encourages shallow root growth, and overwatering leaches valuable nitrogen from the soil and turns the lawn a yellowish-green. The USDA recommends soaking the lawn to a depth of six inches, which should take between one and two inches of water over the lawn surface; then don't water again until the lawn needs it. This encourages the roots to grow deep.

FERTILIZING

How much you need to improve your soil depends on the state of affairs when you take over. If your new turf is growing a healthy garden—or even a healthy weed crop—you may not need to do much at all. However, all soils benefit from the addition of fertilizer. The best way to determine your needs is to get a free soil analysis from your local Cooperative Extension Service (see pages 215–16). They'll also recommend how to improve your soil condition and what will grow best in it.

Commercial fertilizers combine nitrogen, phosphorus, and potassium. A three-number code indicates their proportions. If your plants need help with their leaves, the first number should be high; if it's flowering that needs a boost, a high second number is best; and if the root systems need strengthening, the third number should be highest. Lawn fertilizers usually are highest in nitrogen, and fertilizers for vegetables tend to be high in phosphoric oxide.

Here's a rundown of the different types of fertilizers:

- Organic—made from plant and animal waste, releases nutrient value gradually and unpredictably, usually in summer warmth, when you may not want to fertilize.

- Soluble synthetics—because they dissolve in water, nutrients are made instantly available and a quick green-up can result. To avoid fertilizer burn, apply when the lawn is dry, then thoroughly water as soon as possible after fertilizing.

- Slow release—combine the characteristics of organic and soluble synthetic fertilizers. These are heavy in nitrogen—both water-soluble and water-insoluble—providing slow and fast release of nitrogen.

- Fertilizer/pesticide combinations—a nice idea, killing two birds with one stone, but the right time to feed your lawn and plants is not always the best time to kill insects.

- The best fertilizer for your garden can't be bought; it's the compost you can create from your kitchen waste. Mix lawn clippings and leaves with your organic kitchen scraps. Turn it every few weeks and in six months you'll have valuable food for your lawn and garden. Composting is a disintegration process caused by bacteria and fungus organisms. This results in a considerable reduction in bulk, which may be helpful if you have large amounts of organic refuse and a relatively small area to spread it. There is usually no objectionable odor during the process when layers of soil are added to the pile. This method of recycling waste into dark, rich humus lies at the heart of organic gardening.

GROUND COVERS—THE PROBLEM SOLVERS

Ground covers are ideal for lazy gardeners and a solution to many lawn problems. They include:

- any low-growing plant
- most vines

- prostrate forms of conifers, broad- and narrow-leaf evergreens
- some annual and perennial herbaceous plants

Low-growing plants can solve many landscaping problems. They:

- cover bare spots in the yard
- prevent soil erosion
- regulate foot traffic
- tie together unrelated plants into a composition
- may serve as a fire-retarding screen in arid regions
- filter out dust particles from the air
- hide litter that might blow into your yard
- can be used in areas such as steeply sloping banks, inner courtyards, rock gardens, and areas of dense shade where no other kind of plant or artificial cover can be used

The Advantages of Ground Covers

Regardless of what plant you select, you will find that they are all handled very much alike for site, soil preparation, planting procedures, watering and fertilizing, over-winter care, and yearly management.

A well-established ground cover planting usually needs little maintenance. Occasional fertilizing, mulching, weeding, and watering are the main requirements. (Establishing ground covers, however, takes time. Regardless of the site selected, the soil must be modified to support root growth. However, once established, you're launched.)

TREES

Not even the trees on your property are maintenance-free. But at least they don't need much. Besides occasional fertilizing and spraying, pruning keeps them healthy. Corrective pruning while a tree is young will save difficult and expensive pruning later. Annually check for and remove the following:

- dead, dying, or unsightly limbs
- sprouts and side shoots that grow at or near the base of the tree
- branches that grow from another branch back toward the center of the tree
- branches that cross each other (remove one branch)—disease and decay can enter through abrasions where they rub
- vee crotches (remove one trunk if possible)—they have a tendency to split easily, especially during storms
- nuisance growth—branches that block views, interfere with power or telephone lines, cut off breezes, etc.

More About Pruning

- To make a proper cut, cut close to the branch or branchlet from which the part is to be removed; never leave a stub.
- Pruning cuts, especially larger ones, should be treated with a tree-wound antiseptic (available in either spray or spread-on form).
- Prune during dormancy—in the fall after the leaves have fallen, during the winter; or in early spring before growth starts.

Note: Treatment of splitting trunks, top pruning of tall trees, and felling of diseased or unwanted trees are best left to professional tree surgeons, who have the expertise and equipment you don't.

Householders can be held responsible for destruction of neighboring land by overhanging branches or encroaching roots. The distance to which roots will spread is assumed to equal the eventual height of the tree, although some extend farther. Roots can create cracks in walls and clog drainage pipes. Keep this in mind when you're planting.

Dwarfed Fruit Trees

If your landscape plans call for more trees, consider dwarfed fruit trees. These have several advantages:

- They can be grown in a small area that a larger tree would overfill (thirty or forty dwarf fruit trees can be planted in the space usually taken by three or four regular trees).

- They produce full-grown fruit (each tree provides at least a bushel) and start producing sooner.

- Harvesting is easier and more efficient since no ladders are necessary, and spot picking can be done, with only the properly matured fruit harvested each time.

GARDENING

Over half of America's households grow something, if only herbs and a few tomatoes. In 1982 about thirty-eight million American households tended vegetable gardens, and if one includes those who limit their gardening to flower growing or lawn care, then 86 percent of Americans are gardeners and home gardening is the nation's number one outdoor activity.

If your first house is proving a financial burden, then a vegetable garden may be just the ticket to save money. For the beginner, we recommend restricting your first crops to safe bets such as tomatoes, peas, and squash (especially zucchini). Branch off into more temperamental species as you get better. Another suggestion is to landscape your yard with fruit or nut trees and bushes instead of with decorative plants. Scatter plants around the yard—strawberries along the fence or walk, tomatoes by the southern side of the house, etc. Do a garden later, when you've had experience with a few crops.

Intensive Gardening

No longer is it necessary to allot a sizable chunk of turf for a vegetable patch. Even the virgin homeowner with a postage-stamp-size lawn can break ground for a garden. New techniques maximize annual food production from every square foot of growing space and reduce the amount of unproductive bare ground to an absolute minimum.

- Space is consolidated by planting wide rows instead of the traditional single line of seeds.

- Sprawling ground crops are grown up instead of along the ground.

- Raised permanent beds can counter soil or sloping-ground problems and make harvesting easier.

- Intercropping—mixing two or more similar crops in the same planting bed—improves total yield and combats pest attacks.

- Organic mulches—everything from shredded leaves to newspapers—protect the soil, reduce evaporative moisture loss, and do away with weeding.

- Successive planting—as one crop is harvested another replaces it—keeps gardens producing much of the year.

This concentrated gardening saves time and money. It means less weeding, using fewer commercial fertilizers and pesticides and less irrigation water, and eliminates the need for cumbersome tools such as power garden tillers. Well worth considering!

The Herb Garden
Even if you're not ready to grow your own food, consider growing your own seasonings. Food tastes better with fresh herbs. Here's information to get you started.

Ten herbs that are equally at home inside on a windowsill or outside in a garden are:

- Chives
- Chervil
- Sweet marjoram
- Oregano
- French sorrel
- English thyme
- Basil
- Rosemary
- Parsley
- Savory

Following is a list of a good variety of herbs recommended for beginners:

- Strong herbs—winter savory, rosemary, sage
- Herbs strong enough for accent—sweet basil, dill, mint, sweet marjoram, tarragon, thyme
- Herbs for blending—chives, parsley, summer savory

Herbs can be annuals, biennials, or perennials. Keep these classifications in mind when selecting herbs to grow for the first time.

- Annuals (bloom one season and die)—anise, basil, chervil, coriander, dill, summer savory
- Biennials (live two seasons, blooming second season only) —caraway, parsley
- Perennials (live indefinitely; bloom each season once established)—chives, fennel, lovage, marjoram, mint, tarragon, thyme, winter savory

TO LEARN MORE ABOUT GARDENING

Agencies and Foundations
USDA Cooperative Extension Service

The United States Department of Agriculture has about 3,150 extension service offices spread throughout the fifty states. Local agents will analyze soil, identify insects and diseases, and recommend the best plants for your geographical location. They also sponsor a Master Gardener Program in which local amateur gardeners are trained to go into the community and help other gardeners with their problems. And besides a wide range of publications (among them a comprehensive eight-booklet Home Garden Kit, available for $5.50 from your local agent or the Office of Governmental and Public Affairs, USDA, Washington, DC 20250), most offices have a home economist who will give instruction in everything from canning to first aid.

To find the extension program and Master Gardener Program nearest you, look in the White Pages under County

Extension Office, or USDA Extension Service in the Yellow Pages under the county government listings, or write to the agricultural college of your state university.

Gardens for All
180 Flynn Ave.
Burlington, VT 05401

The director of Gardens for All aims for a return to you of at least ten times the cash you put into your garden. The group's newsletter, *Gardens for All* (The National Association of Gardening News), is published quarterly; annual membership and the newsletter cost $10.00.

Garden Way Publishers
c/o Storey Communications
Rt. 1, Box 105
Pownal, VT 05261

Not only does Garden Way offer a free catalog, it also distributes a line of books, periodicals, tools, and services. Anyone interested in gardening should check out what they have to offer.

Rodale Press
33 E. Minor St.
Emmaus, PA 18049

Rodale publishes *Organic Gardening* magazine. A year's subscription costs $10.00. Rodale is one of the pioneers of the home gardening movement. Among its books is *The Encyclopedia of Organic Gardening* (1,236 pages, $21.95 postpaid). (Also see page 218.)

The Progressive Gardening Institute
c/o National Fulfillment Headquarters
P.O. Box 500
Morrison, TN 37357

Their nursery bulb and seed catalog is free for the asking, and brochures on many gardening subjects are available for a quarter apiece or free with an order.

The National Arbor Day Foundation
Arbor Lodge
Nebraska City, NE 68410

Arbor Day got its start in Nebraska City, and these people started it. Naturally, their brochures and nursery catalog concentrate on trees, though they do get a bit closer to the ground with grape vines, berry plants, and vegetables.

Free Garden Catalogs (Flowers and Vegetables)

Yours for the price of a postcard. But remember, anything you purchase should be compatible with your soil and climate.

Alberta Nurseries & Seeds Ltd.
Box 20
Bowden, AB T0M 0K0
Canada

Bluestone Perennials
7231 Middle Ridge
Madison, OH 44057

Broom Seed Co., Inc.
P.O. Box 236
Rion, SC 29132

W. Atlee Burpee Co.
300 Park Ave.
Warminster, PA 18974

Comstock, Ferre & Co.
263 Main St.
Wethersfield, CT 06109

Henry Field Seed and Nursery Co.
407 Sycamore St.
Shenandoah, IA 51601

Gurney Seed & Nursery Co.
Yankton, SD 57079

Joseph Harris Seed Co.
Moreton Farm
Rochester, NY 14624

Herbst Brothers Seedsmen, Inc.
1000 N. Main St.
Brewster, NY 10509

J.W. Jung Seed Co.
Randolph, WI 53956

Lakeland Nurseries Sales
Hanover, PA 17331

Earl May Seed & Nursery Co.
100 North Elm St.
Shenandoah, IA 51601

Musser Forests, Inc.
Box 340
Indiana, PA 15701

George W. Park Seed Co., Inc.
Greenwood, SC 29647

Pinetree Seed Co.
P.O. Box 1399
Portland, ME 04104

Spruce Brook Nurseries
Box 295
Litchfield, CT 06759

Stark Bros. Nurseries &
   Orchards Co.
Louisiana, MO 63353

Stokes Seeds
Box 548
Buffalo, NY 14240

Thompson & Morgan
P.O. Box 100
Farmingdale, NJ 07727

Urban Farmer, Inc.
22000 Halburton Rd.
Beachwood, OH 44122

Vermont Bean Seed Co.
Garden Lane
Bomoseen, VT 05732

Vesey's Seeds Ltd.
York, P.E.I. C0A 1P0
Canada

Books

One area in which there is no shortage of books is gardening.

There are two encyclopedia gardening books. One is *Rodale's Encyclopedia of Organic Gardening* (1,236 pages); the other is *Wyman's Gardening Encyclopedia* (1,221 pages, $29.95). Both books weigh over a pound and are very thorough. See page 216 for Rodale Press; write to Macmillan Publishing Co., Inc., 866 Third Ave., New York, NY 10022 for *Wyman's Gardening Encyclopedia.*

Reader's Digest Association has published a 672-page oversized hardcover called *Illustrated Guide to Gardening* that is as thorough and well illustrated as their books usually are. It is available from Reader's Digest Association, Pleasantville, NY 10570 for $20.97 plus $1.55 shipping and handling.

Time-Life publishes a thirty-volume series that offers information on the cultivation of indoor and outdoor plants and explains the principles of garden design. The per-volume price is $10.95 plus $2.23 shipping and handling. For information write to Reader Information, Time-Life Books, 541 N. Fairbanks Ct., Chicago, IL 60611.

Ortho Books, a subsidiary of Chevron Chemical Company, has an excellent series of dozens of titles, all priced at about $4.95 apiece. Everything from *All About Pruning* to *The World of Cactus & Succulents* has been thoroughly examined, often regionally. For a free catalog write to Chevron, Ortho Books, Box 3744, San Francisco, CA 94119.

Consumer Guide/Publications International Ltd. has its fine *Vegetable Gardening Encyclopedia—Growing, Freezing, Canning, Drying, Storing.* There's also a special section on herbs as well as recipes for all seasons. Very to the point and highly readable, though far from encyclopedic. Available from Galahad Books, 95 Madison Ave., New York, NY 10016.

The Gardeners Catalogue 2—A Complete Compendium for Indoor, Outdoor, Hydroponic, and Greenhouse Gardeners is *The Whole Earth Catalog* of gardening. The publishers claim it is "the most important gardening tool since the watering can." It's the same size as *The Whole Earth Catalog* and an engrossing volume. Well worth the $12.95 and available from Quill, 105 Madison Ave., New York, NY 10016.

These are just the tip of the iceberg. Literally any gardening subject you need information on has a book about it. Cornell University Press publishes *Dwarfed Fruit Trees* (it's $32.50; write to 124 Roberts Place, Ithaca, NY 14850); Houghton Mifflin (shipping address: Wayside Road, Burlington, MA 01803) will send you *Duane Newcomb's Postage Stamp Garden Book* for $5.95; among Garden Way's many titles (see page 216) is *Carrots Love Tomatoes: Secrets of Companion Planting for Successful Gardening* ($5.95); and Rodale (see page 216) has its *Color Handbook of Garden Insects* by Anna Carr for $12.95. Check your local library and bookstores for these and more!

Chapter 10

THE VACATION OR WEEKEND HOME

"Part time" houses have their special problems. Many people purchase a house that was once lived in year round, and the first time they shut it down for a season they return to find that the paint is peeling from the ceiling; the chimney soot, accumulated over four decades, has come loose and fallen into the furnace; and a toilet that needed jiggling kept the water pump running until it burned out. It is essential that houses be properly left to themselves—whether for a week or for a year —so they won't self-destruct.

If you are the virgin homeowner of a vacation or weekend house, use the checklist we provide here to get yourself started, then make adjustments to suit your needs. The important thing is to have a checklist so when you're fifty miles down the pike, heading back home for the winter, you won't start wondering whether you locked the windows or suddenly remember that you forgot to close the damper on the fireplace.

The special security problems for the second house, many

of which apply when you're on vacation, are covered on page 28 in Chapter 2: "Safety and Security."

OPENING A SUMMER HOUSE

Before Arriving

- Have the phone, electricity, gas, and water turned on.

- If possible, have a cleaning expedition and perform everything listed below. It will make your arrival with family and luggage much easier.

- If you're unable to make a special cleaning trip, pack sufficient food and drink to tide you over until you can get out to go shopping.

- Arrange for your mail to be forwarded to the new location.

Upon Arrival

- Check and order bottled gas or other fuel.

- Are there any rodent traps that need checking and emptying?

- Turn on appliances and make sure they're working properly.

- Ignite pilot lights if you use them. (They can be turned off by a professional, then you can use matches to light burners. The saving in gas is hefty.)

- Check pressure gauges on fire extinguishers. Test smoke detectors. (See pages 22–25).

- Check the boiler water and turn on the boiler. (See also pages 165–74 on heating systems.)

- Check the well; clean and oil the water pump. (For more about freshwater systems, see pages 157–65.)

- Inspect the pipes for leaks and corrosion.

- Have the chimney checked. Does it need cleaning? Is it clogged by nests? (See pages 82–83 and 184–87.)

- Does the thermostat have a clock? Multiple settings (for day, night, weekends)? Reset it. (See page 177.)
- Reset the clocks.
- Remove storm windows and any protective window coverings in all except air-conditioned rooms.
- Clean the windows before putting up the screens.
- Check the fans. Clean and give them a shot of oil, if possible. (See pages 175–76.)
- Check the air-conditioners. Make sure the filters are clean. (See pgs. 174–75.)
- Open the windows and air out the house.
- Air out the bedding, mattresses, and cushions.
- Remove cobwebs and clean the house completely—dust, vacuum, mop, wash, etc.
- Wash the drapes and spreads.
- Check the ceilings and look in the attic. Are there signs that the roof has been leaking? Do any other repairs need to be made to the house, inside or out? Arrange to have work done that you can't handle yourself. Give the leaks priority.
- Unpack.
- Make the beds. Put out fresh towels.
- Make a shopping list.
- Shop for food, household supplies.
- Notify neighbors, post office, police, and stores of your arrival.
- Arrange for garbage pickup and/or get a town dump sticker.
- Get town passes, permits, and beach stickers.
- Arrange for deliveries such as newspapers.
- Get out the lawn mower and rakes; get the yard in shape. (More about lawn mowers and mowing on pages 203–8.)

- Open outdoor electrical outlets; uncover outdoor sockets; put in light bulbs or floodlights.
- Check the awnings. Will they survive the season? Set them up.
- Take out the lawn furniture, grill (check charcoal), yard swings, hammocks, equipment for children, etc.
- Set up the clothesline.
- Clean and oil the pool pump; uncover, clean, and fill the swimming pool.
- Check out the dock or float for strength and safety. Secure any loose planks and replace any rotten ones. Is there a life buoy that can be thrown to a swimmer in trouble? Anchor the floating dock or platform.
- Check the sports equipment—badminton and croquet sets, tennis rackets, golf clubs, etc. Inflate rafts, bicycle tires, and the like.
- Clean out the boat. Give it a fresh painting if necessary. What about safety equipment? Are life jackets and boat cushions in good condition? Will the motor start right up? Launch!
- Review safety rules with the kids. Stress what to do in case of fire and in case someone falls overboard. Are phone numbers of the fire department and of the nearest doctor and hospital posted by the phone? They should be.
- Are roof gutters and drains free of leaves? (See pages 142–48 for cleaning and repairing them.)
- While you're on a ladder, check the roof flashing. (See pages 190–91.)
- If you banked or mulched shrubbery, uncover it.
- Check the crawl space under the house. Are there signs of termites or other bug infestation? Any rot or decay? Take care of any of these problems if you find them. (See pages 191–95.)
- Start a garden.

CLOSING DOWN A SUMMER HOUSE

What Can Be Done Ahead of Time

- The last time you use the lawn mower, garden hoses, outdoor grill, and other yard items, put them away. Drain gasoline out of the lawn mower. Drain water out of the hose. Store charcoal in a dry place.
- Arrange that newspaper, mail, and other deliveries be stopped the day of your departure. The phone should be disconnected and the garbage collected for the last time the day after you leave.
- Check the house for needed repairs and arrange to have work done.
- Get cartons for packing.
- Arrange for winter watch of your house with neighbors and/or police. Leave the keys with any you trust. (Also see pages 27–28.)
- Return any borrowed items or library books.
- Pick up clothes from the laundry or dry cleaner.
- Start planning your meals so you can eat the food on hand.
- Defrost the refrigerator.
- Mulch around plants and shrubs.
- Repair screens. (For how to do this, see pages 131–33.)

The Last Few Days

- Deflate, disassemble, and put away rafts and other sports gear such as swings, children's equipment, etc.
- Drain the pump; empty, clean, and cover the swimming pool.
- Put away the boat.
- Pull the dock or float out of the water.
- Cover or remove the air-conditioners.

- Outdoor light bulbs should be removed and all light sockets and electrical outlets covered.
- Remove the awnings and store them in a dry place.
- Make sure roof gutters and drains are free of debris. (See pages 142–48.)
- Drain the outside water faucets if you don't drain the entire system.
- Any spreads, rugs, or drapes that need cleaning should be removed and taken care of.
- Dismantle any items that go with you.

The Day of Departure

- Put away, camphorize, or mothball blankets, linens, and bedding.
- Take down the clothesline. Take in all lawn furniture. Give the yard a once-over to make sure nothing has been left out and that everything is in order.
- Close the chimney damper and clean out the fireplace. (See pages 184–87.)
- If you keep valuables such as televisions, stereos, even liquor, store and lock them up.
- Check drawers, closets, and hampers.
- Pack.
- Don't leave anything for rodents; remove all perishable food items. Set a few traps if rodents are a nuisance.
- Give the house a light cleaning.
- Remove the screens. Put up storm windows and doors and any protective window and door coverings.
- Lock all the windows.
- Shut down the boiler. Reset the thermostat.
- Turn off the water and drain the pipes; shut down the hot-water heater and drain it.

- Can the cellar door into the house be locked? If your basement is vulnerable to break-in, a hand-operated dead-bolt lock on that door is a good idea.
- Turn off the gas.
- Whether or not you shut off the electricity, make sure all appliances are disconnected, including clocks and the fridge. Leave the refrigerator door open.
- Turn out the lights and turn off the electricity.
- Set the alarm system.
- Lock the house, the garage, and sheds.

THE WEEKEND HOUSE

Leaving It

Leaving the weekend house is not so difficult; however, certain checks must be made before taking off.

- Make sure the thermostat is turned down. It's a huge waste of energy to heat an empty house five days a week.
- Do you have any warning systems installed in case your boiler breaks down in a hard freeze? If so, set them. (Note: Honeywell makes a Winter Watchman that turns on a light for a neighbor to see when the temperature drops below a certain point. Robertshaw manufactures a room thermostat that hooks to the telephone and engages your phone when the house temperature drops; if you call and get a busy signal, you know the boiler has failed.)
- Turn the hot-water heater off; otherwise it wastes a lot of electricity reheating water that won't be used until the next weekend.
- Check that all individual electric heaters are unplugged. Many operate on thermostats and might turn on as the house cools down.
- Double-check that all windows and doors, including screen doors, are locked.
- Close the fireplace dampers. (See pages 184–86.)

- If you have a timer that turns lights on and off, make sure it's set; otherwise, all lights should be turned off. That includes basement, attic, closets, garage, tool sheds, and any other lights that are easily forgotten.

- If you have a dead-bolt lock on the cellar door, lock it. It's a good idea to have one if your cellar might be easy to break into.

- Close some but not all window shades, blinds, or curtains. (You don't want your house to look abandoned.) Those that get summer sun should be drawn to prevent the fading of rugs, carpeting, upholstery, and other fabrics. If you have venetian blinds: In the winter, turn the vents up; this keeps heat inside the house while also admitting radiant heat from the sun; in the summer, turn the vents down; the blinds then act as insulating barriers to the sun.

- In winter keep the doors to unheated rooms closed and open them to heated rooms, especially bathrooms, to allow even exchange of air.

- Never leave a clothes dryer going—if it accidentally doesn't shut off it can set a house on fire. And keep the dryer door closed in winter, otherwise it lets in cool air through its exhaust.

- In summer, remove all lawn furniture and make sure that anything left outside is secured.

- If you have a phone answering machine to take messages for you during the week, turn it on.

- Give the fridge a once-over. Take all food that might go bad during the week.

- Don't leave garbage inside.

- Check that all water taps are closed and that toilets are not running. Before you leave, stop! The water pump should not be operating. If you hear it running, wait for it to shut off.

- Lock up the house, the garage, sheds, etc.

- Set the alarm system.

Appendix

WHERE TO FIND MORE INFORMATION

U.S. GOVERNMENT PRINTING OFFICE

The GPO, with over twenty-five thousand publications and periodicals for sale, is one of the best sources of low-cost information. To keep it all manageable, the material is broken down by subject. Write for "The Home" subject biography —literally every aspect of homeowning is included. Or if you want the whole picture, request *A Consumer's Guide to Federal Publications,* their free subject index. Prices of the publications themselves start at about $1.00.

This takes time. If you're lucky, things will go faster at your local GPO bookstore. It stocks many titles and has access to all the rest. Boston, Cleveland, Columbus, Dallas, Denver, Detroit, Jacksonville, Los Angeles, New York, Philadelphia, Pueblo, San Francisco, and Seattle all have GPO bookstores.

Besides the free subject index catalog of federal publications mentioned above, there's also another for posters, charts, and pictures (No. SB-057). In addition, there is a free monthly catalog, *Selected U.S. Government Publications,* which contains only the new and consistently popular items.

All of the catalogs are available from the Superintendent of Documents, U.S. Government Printing Office, Washington, DC 20402.

CONSUMER INFORMATION CENTER

Then there's the General Services Administration, which distributes over two hundred publications, over half of which are

228

free. A free catalog, updated quarterly, is available from the Consumer Information Center and has a complete housing section.

Send a card to Consumer Information Center, Distribution Center, Pueblo, CO 81009.

CONSUMERS UNION

With the increased space and increased maintenance of a home, you're going to be investing in more and more consumer items, and what you don't know can hurt you. It's hard to find real value without objective guidance, no matter how carefully you read labels, listen to salespeople, or compare prices. *Consumer Reports* has rated virtually everything from roofing materials and refrigerators to floor varnishes and lawn mowers. Check back issues in your library before buying anything major, or subscribe by writing to *Consumer Reports,* Subscription Department, Box 1959, Marion, OH 43306.

CR is published by Consumers Union, a nonprofit group that has worked since 1936 to inform consumers about what they'll get for their money and to create and maintain decent living standards for consumers. It maintains law offices in Washington, D.C., San Francisco, and Austin, and initiates lawsuits and petitions to government agencies on behalf of consumers.

Among Consumers Union's other publications is *Penny Power,* a consumer magazine for kids 8 to 12, intended to offset some of the influence of commercials and to help develop good consumer attitudes and buying habits.

Consumer Reports Books produces paperback books on a wide variety of topics, including *Guide to Energy in the Home* and *Whole House Catalog* (a how-to book featuring brand-name product recommendations). Consumers Union also publishes an annual *Buying Guide.* For more information about Consumers Union and its publications, write to Office of Public Information, Consumers Union, Mount Vernon, NY 10553.

CORNELL UNIVERSITY

Hundreds of booklets covering a wide range of topics in the areas of home energy, maintenance, and ecology are available for $0.60 and up from Cornell University. Write to Cornell University Distribution Center, 7 Research Park, Ithaca, NY 14850, for their free "Know How" catalog listing available titles.

NATIONAL PLAN SERVICE

This service has pamphlets—usually priced at about $1.25—for almost every home repair, home project, or room plan (if you're remodeling or adding on). Many publications give only an overview, but National Plan Service gets down to basics. Get their free catalog by sending a card to 435 W. Fullerton Ave., Elmhurst, IL 60126.

BETTER BUSINESS BUREAU

If you're wondering about the reputation of a contractor, an appliance dealer and its service department, or anyone else you may want to do business with, try your local Better Business Bureau. They won't give you recommendations, but they will tell you if a firm has any record of complaints and angry customers.

They also publish *Better Business Bureau Guide to Wise Buying* ($7.95). It gives basic advice on purchasing common goods and services, as well as warnings about common scams and swindles. For the book, or for a listing of free pamphlets that cover about the same ground, write to the Council of Better Business Bureaus, Inc., 1515 Wilson Blvd., Suite 300, Arlington, VA 22209.

YOUR LOCAL UTILITY

Don't overlook the information and services relating to conservation and energy resources available from your local utility. Most electric companies have a library of free pamphlets and, if you're lucky, they'll also have energy auditors who will visit and evaluate your home's energy situation. Be prepared for a combination of sound advice and self-excusing propaganda. Contact the customer service department or public information department.

THE EDISON FOUNDATION

The Thomas Alva Edison Foundation offers books that will help your children understand why insulation is important, how much energy it takes to heat water, and how much hot water normal household tasks consume. Be prepared for strange boxes in your refrigerator and footsteps in the attic— but maybe they'll start turning off the lights. Booklets are $0.50 each; three are $1.00. Bulk rates are available for classes and groups. Write to the foundation at Cambridge Office Plaza, Suite 141, 18280 W. 10 Mile Road, Southfield, MI 48075.

BOOKS OF INTEREST

There are scores of books in the home section of every bookstore and library. The names of the books cannot be listed here, but rest assured that there is a book or pamphlet available on any aspect of home repair, furnishing, or remodeling you want to do.

Sunset Books has forty-seven books on home improvement and building; of these, thirty-five deal with indoor projects and twelve, with outdoor. They're highly informative and well worth the $3.95 to $5.95 prices. Write for their free catalog to Sunset Books, Willow and Middlefield Road, Menlo Park, CA 94025.

Reader's Digest Association publishes three excellent, easy-to-understand, well-illustrated do-it-yourself and fix-it-yourself books: *The Reader's Digest Complete Do-It-Yourself Manual, The Reader's Digest Complete Fix-It-Yourself Manual,* and *The*

Reader's Digest Home Improvement Manual. All are available at your local library, bookstore, or through Reader's Digest Books, Pleasantville, NY 10570. The fix-it-yourself and do-it-yourself books are $18.99 a piece plus $1.55 postage and handling; the home improvement book is $19.95 plus $1.32 postage and handling.

Time-Life has a thirty-six-volume set of home books. Though a little pricey, you name it, they cover it. Each book is between 170 and 190 pages, and the cost is $9.95 plus $2.23 handling. Write to Time-Life at 541 N. Fairbanks Ct., Chicago, IL 60611 for a listing.

If you run up against "They don't make that anymore," you probably can use *The Old-House Journal Catalog,* which lists more than twelve hundred companies that sell over nine thousand individual items and services. It's updated annually and is available from *The Old-House Journal* for $11.95. Subscribers can order it for $9.95. *The Old-House Journal* is published ten times a year and deals with the restoration and maintenance of old houses. Write them at 69A Seventh Ave., Brooklyn, NY 11217.

Your Guide to Free Energy Information by Arthur Liebers is a 128-page paperback sourcebook of reliable and free energy conservation information organizing hundreds of brochures, pamphlets, folders, and fliers. It gives a brief description of each, with addresses and phone numbers, and is well worth the price. From Delair Publishing Co., Inc., 420 Lexington Ave., New York, NY 10170. The book costs $2.95 postpaid.

Conserving Energy in Older Homes, a well-illustrated book for those with homes built before 1950, was originally published by the Department of Housing and Urban Development. Though federal budget cuts canceled further printings of the book, editor Jeffrey Seisler felt it important enough to be kept on the market—and he's right. Order it by mail for $4.95 plus $0.65 postage from Analytech, Suite C-30, 915 King St., Alexandria, VA 22314.

INDEX